ADVENTURE *Awaits*

Adventure Awaits

Published by Applesauce Press, an imprint of HarperCollins Focus LLC, 501 Nelson Place, Nashville, TN 37214 USA.

13-Digit ISBN: 978-1-40034-716-2
10-Digit ISBN: 1-40034-716-5

Books published by Applesauce Press Book Publishers are available at special discounts for bulk purchases in the United States by corporations, institutions, and other organizations. For more information, please contact the publisher.

cidermillpress.com

HarperCollins Publishers, Macken House, 39/40 Mayor Street Upper, Dublin 1, D01 C9W8, Ireland (https://www.harpercollins.com)

Typography: Azo Sans, SantElia Rough, Veneer
Image Credits: Image on page 43 used under official license from Shutterstock.com. All other photography courtesy of Ky Furneaux.
All illustrations courtesy of Cider Mill Press.

Printed in Bosnia and Herzegovina

25 26 27 28 29 GPS 5 4 3 2 1

First Edition

ADVENTURE Awaits

THE BEGINNER'S GUIDE TO THE GREAT OUTDOORS

Ky Furneaux

TABLE OF Contents

1 INTRO TO SURVIVAL • 8

2 ATTITUDES OF SURVIVAL • 10

3 HOW TO PREVENT SURVIVAL SCENARIOS • 16

4 THE BASIC NEEDS OF SURVIVAL • 22

KNIVES • 26

A RULES FOR USING A BLADE • 28
B HOW TO USE A KNIFE • 29
C STUCK WITHOUT A BLADE? • 32
D KNIFE ACTIVITIES • 34
E SURVIVAL MYTHS ABOUT KNIVES • 40

SHELTER • 42

A LESSONS FROM THE PAST • 42
B WHY SHELTER IS IMPORTANT • 43
C CHOOSING YOUR SHELTER LOCATION • 44
D PROPERTIES OF A GOOD SHELTER • 46
E DIFFERENT TYPES OF SURVIVAL SHELTERS • 47
F KNOTS • 54
G TARP SHELTERS • 56
H SHELTER ACTIVITIES • 58
I SURVIVAL MYTHS ABOUT SHELTER BUILDING • 62

WATER • 64

A LESSONS FROM THE PAST • 64
B WHY WATER IS IMPORTANT • 64
C HOW TO FIND WATER IN THE OUTDOORS • 67
D COLLECTING WATER • 68
E MAKING WATER SAFE TO DRINK • 72
F WATER ACTIVITIES • 76
G SURVIVAL MYTHS ABOUT WATER • 80

FIRE • 82

A LESSONS FROM THE PAST • 82
B WHY FIRE IS IMPORTANT • 83
C HOW TO BE SAFE WITH FIRE • 84
D PREPARATION FOR FIRE MAKING • 85
E THE FIRE MAKING POSITION • 91
F BEST METHODS OF FIRE MAKING • 92
G ACTIVITIES TO PRACTICE MAKING FIRE • 106
H SURVIVAL MYTHS ABOUT FIRE • 112

9

FOOD • 114

A LESSONS FROM THE PAST • 114
B SURVIVAL FOODS • 115
C HUNTING • 128
D PREPARING WILD FOOD • 143
E ACTIVITIES TO PRACTICE FOR OBTAINING WILD FOODS • 146
F SURVIVAL MYTHS ABOUT FOOD • 151

RESCUE • 152

A LESSONS FROM THE PAST • 152
B THE BEST WAYS TO GET RESCUED • 153
C NAVIGATION • 157
D ACTIVITIES TO PRACTICE FOR RESCUE • 163
E SURVIVAL MYTHS ABOUT RESCUE • 166

BASIC WILDERNESS FIRST AID • 168

A LESSONS FROM THE PAST • 168
B DRSABC • 169
C DEADLY BLEEDS AND WOUNDS • 175
D BREAKS AND SPRAINS • 177
E BITES AND STINGS • 177
F HEAT AND COLD INJURIES • 179
G SPLINTS • 183
H EVACUATION • 184
I WHAT'S IN YOUR FIRST AID KIT? • 187
J FIRST AID ACTIVITIES • 189
K SURVIVAL MYTHS ABOUT FIRST AID • 191

QUIZ: WOULD YOU SURVIVE? • 194

INTRO TO SURVIVAL

Welcome to the exciting world of survival knowledge!

If you're holding this book, chances are you're curious and adventurous. You probably enjoy the outdoors or want to spend more time out there safely. You're not content with sitting back and watching life pass you by. You want to experience *everything* the world has to offer.

Life can throw us curveballs. And the best way to deal with those curveballs is to learn how to catch them. Whether your curveball looks like getting lost on a hike, facing a natural disaster, or simply finding yourself in a sticky situation, knowing how to survive and being prepared to do so is an essential skill for anyone who wants to live life to the fullest.

That's where this book comes in!

It's packed with practical advice, real-life stories, and step-by-step instructions on everything from developing good preparation practices and building a shelter to finding food and water in the wild. I've spent my life exploring some of the most remote corners of the globe, and I've put my body on the line to test every bit of knowledge in this book. I know how to enable you to make proactive decisions when seconds and minutes count.

I've also included a few practical activities to work through along with challenging, multiple-choice scenarios to see if you could make the best decisions for your survival. By the time you get done with this book, I know you'll be feeling a lot more confident about your time in the outdoors.

So, whether you're planning a weekend camping trip or simply want to be prepared for whatever life throws your way, this book is your ultimate guide to surviving and thriving in the great outdoors. Let's get started!

2

ATTITUDES OF SURVIVAL

Although there are many useful habits and attitudes that can help you in emergency situations and everyday life, I have pinpointed the four that I think are the most important to help get you through. They are:

BE POSITIVE **BE PREPARED**

BE EDUCATED **BE ADAPTABLE**

Simple, right? Although people tell us to adopt these attitudes all the time, they never really explain *how* to develop them. I've learned these attitudes are like muscles. If you use them, they'll grow to be part of how you deal with problems. But if you don't, they are easy to forget.

Here are a few pointers to make these attitudes part of your everyday life.

BE POSITIVE

In survival scenarios, the hardest thing to fight against is fear and hopelessness. They are normal feelings. You may be in a very unpredictable and possibly frightening place and the hardest thing in the world can be to be proactive and positive. But here are some ways to help you do that:

1. FOCUS ON WHAT YOU CAN CHANGE

Working to make your situation better will help distract you but it will also increase your chances of a successful rescue. Are you cold? Can you get warm? Can you make a shelter? Can you find some cover? Can you make yourself visible to rescuers? What supplies are you carrying? Take stock of the assets you have with you. Are you too hot? Can you find some shade? All these are things that you should be able to do something about and will keep you busy and prevent panic from setting in. Don't dwell on the negatives that you can't do anything about. You may want a hamburger and some fries but wanting them isn't going to make them appear so you will just feel bad that you don't have them. Focus instead on the fact you haven't eaten your banana from lunch and that will help fill your stomach tonight.

2. REMEMBER THE SITUATION IS (PROBABLY) TEMPORARY

In most cases people will get rescued between one to three days of getting lost or ending up in a life-or-death scenario. You can last three days without water and three weeks without food, so chances are you'll be rescued before you need to do more than find a way to stay warm for the night. Your situation may seem awful, but remember that you have the stamina and strength to get through these first survival days, even if you don't feel like you do.

3. RECOGNIZE THAT FEAR IS A RESPONSE TO *PERCEIVED* THREATS

Back in the paleolithic years, the world was abundant with threats to humans. A peek into the wrong cave could result in getting eaten by a saber-toothed tiger. So, we humans evolved to have something called a "flight-or-fight" response. When your brain tells your body there's something you need to worry about, a quick burst of adrenaline shoots through your system. Back then, adrenaline would give your body the strength to outrun the saber-toothed tiger, or even try to fight it. The problem with having such a honed fight-or-flight response today is that there aren't nearly as many physical threats to humans anymore, but your brain still pumps your body full of that adrenaline when you're scared. This adrenaline causes rapid heartbeat, rapid breathing, and sweaty armpits, and makes you hyper-alert to what's going on around you. Just this stress response alone can cause panic if you aren't aware of what's happening.

There may be good reason for this response: if you're in immediate danger, then remove yourself from the danger if you can. But if you can take a moment, analyze the reason for that fight-or-flight response. Are you reacting to a noise you've heard before? A big noise? Is it coming closer or going away? Can you see what's causing the noise? Chances are that that noise could be a little squirrel making its way through the brush, rather than a bear coming to eat you. Running off into the dark and away from the noise could cause you more harm than just staying put and letting the little critter pass by. Small things make big noises in the night, and it's important to not let the fear of the unknown take control.

Another perceived threat could be something you've been taught to fear but isn't actually dangerous. Most spiders are like that. I knew a girl who was terrified of birds but couldn't pinpoint why. In your survival scenario you'll need to rationally look at what you're scared of and decide whether it really *is* a threat to your life or just something you're scared of but won't actually harm you. You may need to take a deep breath and decide to ignore those fears until you are rescued. Your mind is stronger than you think.

BE EDUCATED

Hopefully before you head out into the wilderness, you have learned some things about the area that you are going into—but if your survival situation has come out of the blue as a result of a natural disaster or something unexpected like a plane crash or a car breaking down, then you will need to educate yourself about your surroundings.

Once you have made your way out of potential danger, it's time to take stock of your surroundings. Your best bet for getting rescued is to stay where you are if possible and make yourself as visible as you can.

Have a look around and see if you can identify things as potential assets to your situation. Is there drinkable water nearby? Are you close to a clearing or a hill where you might be more visible to potential rescuers? Is there a naturally formed shelter that could keep you out of the wind and cold? Get a feel for what is close by so you can begin to make your situation better.

BE PREPARED

Once you've found yourself in a disaster scenario, it's time to get prepared for what may come. Hopefully you have had a chance to prepare a little with the kit you have brought with you. But again, your survival scenario may have been something that happened unexpectedly. In these types of completely out-of-the-blue situations, you'll need to start thinking about the next few hours—or even the next few days. What do *you* need to make this situation better? Is it getting dark? If so, you'll need to think about getting some shelter for the night. Is it really hot? You might need to think about where to find drinkable water. Waiting until you're super thirsty will give you brain fog and make you confused, which will make finding and purifying water difficult. And don't wait until you hear the rescue planes to get your signals ready. They should be up, visible, and ready to go at any moment. Be prepared to wait a while for someone to find you, and be prepared to make sure you are ready for any rescue attempt.

BE ADAPTABLE

Along with being resilient, being adaptable is one of the most important survival skills you can have. Being adaptable means that you can problem solve and be flexible with your thinking. A shoelace might be holding your shoe on, but it might also work as a bit of rope if you need to tie something together, or as a piece of cord to help with fire making. You might think that a cave is the ideal shelter, but if the closest thing to you is a hollow tree—it will do. And you may be used to drinking water that is clean and clear out of a tap, but sometimes that puddle of muddy water might be the thing that saves your life.

Another thing that you can be adaptable about is the trash you might find around you. It's hard to go anywhere in the world and not come across man-made rubbish. Collect all you can find, and think about what it may be useful for. A plastic bottle may store rainwater or become a water filter. A piece of glass could become a knife or help start a fire. One person's trash may become a treasure for you.

So get creative out there, and begin to look at everything in the world around you as assets to make you comfortable and keep you healthy.

3

HOW TO PREVENT SURVIVAL SCENARIOS

Preparation can ensure that 50 percent of survival scenarios don't ever eventuate. If you are carrying a charger for your phone, your battery might last long enough to make that emergency call to get help. If your phone has died, but you have a paper copy of the maps with you, these may guide you to your car. Preparation can also be valuable in any unforeseen circumstance that may arise. It's hard to predict natural disasters or accidents. But when you make sure someone knows where you're going and when to expect you back, chances are you can get rescued and be home by dinner if you get lost, rather than having to build a shelter and hope someone figures out where you might be over a series of days.

Any time you decide to take a trip into the outdoors, it's important to **educate yourself** about where you're going and what you'll need to take. This can be as easy as googling a map of the area and checking what the weather will be like when you go. It's important not to rely on technology, as it can fail if you go out of service range or if your battery dies. Instead, print off a paper copy of the map of the area, or grab one from a park office on the way to your location. Look at the terrain around where you'll be, and decide on appropriate clothing, footwear, and provisions.

The next step is to **prepare yourself**. If there's a chance of rain, pack a rain jacket. If the weather is sunny and warm, pack sunscreen, a hat, and more water than you would normally take. All of this seems pretty straightforward, but over a third of first-aid scenarios in Australia (where I'm from!) occur due to heat exhaustion because hikers haven't brought enough water on a hike.

Another vital piece of kit is a **first aid kit**. Seems like extra weight to carry, but if you need it, then a first aid kit can be a lifesaver. I am always surprised at how many people venture into the outdoors without one. A small first aid kit can be the difference between needing to be rescued or being able to walk out. For day trips, my first aid kit is small and terrain-specific. It usually contains at least the following:

- **2 PRESSURE BANDAGES**
- **1 ROLLER BANDAGE**
- **1 TRIANGULAR BANDAGE**
- **GAUZE OR COTTON PADS**
- **STRAPPING TAPE**
- **ADHESIVE DRESSINGS**
- **ANTISEPTIC WIPES**

Later on, in the First Aid chapter, I'll talk about why I choose to bring these items and how to use them.

When you venture outdoors, it's also important to **carry some kind of communication device**. Today cell phones work in most places, but if you're heading into a remote area, consider carrying a satellite phone or some kind of emergency location device. The technology for these devices is rapidly changing, so make sure that you check with your local outdoor provider to find one that suits your needs.

Here's a checklist that will allow you to be adequately prepared for a day trip into the outdoors:

1. **NAVIGATION EQUIPMENT: A GPS, PLUS A PAPER MAP AND A COMPASS**

2. **HEADLAMP AND SPARE BATTERIES**
(I bring this even if I don't plan to be out at night.)

3. **SMALL FIRST AID KIT**

4. **KNIFE**

5. **LIGHTER**

6. **FERRO ROD** (Fire starter)

7. **WHISTLE**

8. **AT LEAST HALF A GALLON OF WATER**
(Drink a good amount before you hike, and refill your bottles before you set off. Being hydrated from the start puts you ahead of the game.)

9. **MEALS, PLUS EXTRA SNACKS**

10. **EXTRA LAYERS OF WARM CLOTHING**
(thermals, beanies, etc.)

11. **WATERPROOF JACKET**

12. **EMERGENCY BIVY BAG OR SMALL TARP**

13. **LIFESTRAW OR WATER PURIFICATION TABLETS**

14. **HAT AND SUNSCREEN**

15. **PHONE AND PORTABLE CHARGER**
(Tip: Make sure the charger is, well, charged!)

It looks like a long list, but it will all fit into a small daypack with ease, and could save your life.

The last part to being prepared (and one of the most important) is to notify a responsible adult of where you're going and how long you plan to go. I usually add a few hours on to the expected walk time to allow for rest breaks or unexpected detours along the way. This way, if something does happen to you on the outing, a rescue party will be on its way swiftly and headed straight to your area. Just remember—it's *really* important to notify that adult once you've returned.

If you take all these steps prior to heading into the outdoors, chances are that you'll be able to competently and efficiently handle most things that nature throws your way. Even if you don't need all of these tips and items to save your life, you may be able to assist those who are in trouble from their lack of preparation.

25 Piece Kit
QuicKit
First Aid on the go!
Trafalgar
3
12
13
2
6
5
7
14
everyday
HENK'S KITCHEN
BILTONG
9

11
Northern Walks
Grampians
National Park
1
GARMIN
Parks
10
15
4
8

THE BASIC NEEDS OF SURVIVAL

The first thing to understand when you're trying to figure out your Survival Needs is the difference between a want and a need. It's pretty simple, really. A **need** is something you will eventually die without, and a **want** is everything else. In life there may be things that feel very important to you (like perhaps your cell phone) but I promise you will not die without them.

Your basic survival needs are shelter, water, fire, and food. I always add rescue into here though, because your aim isn't to be able to last out there indefinitely but to be safely rescued as soon as possible. These Survival Needs are defined loosely by the rule of 3's.

As always, your first priority is to remove yourself from danger, but then you will need to assess your situation according to the following rules:

THE RULE OF 3s

When you find yourself in a survival scenario and need to prioritize your needs, remember the Rule of 3s. This says you can generally last:

3 MINUTES WITHOUT OXYGEN

3 HOURS IN EXTREME TEMPERATURES

3 DAYS WITHOUT WATER

3 WEEKS WITHOUT FOOD

No matter what situation you're in, food is generally the last thing you need to be thinking about. Now, this doesn't seem true when you feel like you're starving if you miss breakfast. But believe me, eating three meals is just a habit your brain will trick you into thinking is an urgent need. So you can put food to the back of your mind for now.

Chances are, your survival scenario won't put you in an oxygen-deprived environment. But if it does, try to get out immediately, as you only have three minutes before you become dysfunctional.

Now you need to decide whether your environment would be classified as "extreme" weather. Although the air might feel nice and warm during the day in a desert, temperatures may plummet to below freezing at night. Are you in a snowy or icy area? Are you exposed to scorching heat? Are you in a rainforest in wet season? If you decide that you're in one of these extreme temperature areas, your priorities will be shelter and, if cold is an issue, fire. If you don't have fire-making tools, don't panic. Just focus your efforts on making a good shelter that will conserve your body heat. The best forms of shelter will be discussed in the Shelter section.

If you feel confident that you can last overnight in your location without spending too much time constructing a solid shelter, start scouting for a good water source. Remember that generally you have three days before you need water, but in hot dry areas or cold windy areas, the environment will suck the moisture from your body and you will need water much sooner. You may be nowhere near a water source, so consider where your closest water source might be prior to building a shelter, as you may need to move to get closer to water.

Once you have assessed the area for these three needs, it is time to look at rescue. Hopefully you prepared well prior to leaving home, so someone will quickly raise the alarm when you don't return on time. To increase your chances of being rescued, you will need to become as visible as possible to people scouting the area.

Again, you will need to make a decision. If nightfall is coming, your priority is to make it through the night if rescue doesn't come. So do what you need to do to ensure that your greatest need (shelter and fire) is met before spending time making your big SOS in the clearing.

These rules may seem confusing, but don't worry—we'll talk about them more in following chapters. By the end of the book, you will be able to assess your survival scenario and make the best decisions in order to make it out alive and well.

5

KNIVES

If I am asked to choose one item to take into an extreme scenario with me, my answer will always be a blade. A sharp and enduring edge is the most useful tool you can have with you but is one of the hardest things to find in an outdoor survival scenario. For this reason, I tend to have a variety of blades scattered throughout my possessions and generally always carry at least one, depending on the activity I am participating in.

Handling knives safely is an important skill to learn, as the wrong cut from a knife can result in serious injury and make your survival situation a lot harder to get through. For this reason, I encourage people to pick up and get used to handling knives from a young age in a safe environment.

Depending on your age, I suggest beginning your knife use with adult supervision. It's important to remember that knives are tools, not toys or weapons. Used in the right way, they can be your most valuable asset. Knives can help you meet all of your survival needs in some way. They can cut wood for fire, create traps for food, cut a digging stick for water and cut vines to make rope for shelters.

When choosing a knife, make sure that the knife fits comfortably in the palm of your hand. Also, the blade should be no longer

than the palm of your hand. Larger knives can be useful in some scenarios, (they are great to help cut down large branches for shelters), but for finer tasks like whittling and carving, large knives can be unwieldly and hard to manage.

There is a misconception that a knife should be blunt for beginners, so they can get used to handling them. Unfortunately, more knife accidents happen with blunt knives than sharp ones. Blunt knives require more force to get the job done, and extra force on a blunt blade in a misguided direction can still cause serious injury. That's why it's important to keep your knife sharp.

A: RULES FOR USING A BLADE

There are a few rules to follow when you're using a knife:

Always cut away from the body and away from the hand that's holding whatever you're working on. Your body has a zone that you need to protect. It's called "the blood triangle" by survival teachers. It consists of your torso and your upper legs. There are arteries in these areas that, if cut, would cause you to bleed out in under two minutes. Your noncutting hand also has a major artery in it at the wrist that can lead to a dangerous bleed if severed. In order to use your knife safely, sit with your knees apart and your elbows propped on your knees. In this position it will make it impossible to accidentally hit the blood triangle. Keep your non-working hand above the cutting blade.

Make sure no one is within reach of your blade while you are using it. Establish a "blood circle." This is the area around your body that you can reach if you put both arms out horizontally and circle them around. Do not use your blade if there is anyone else within your blood circle. Simply sheath the blade until a safe blood circle can be established.

Keep your knife sheathed when not in use. I often see people place their knife beside them when they're not using it. If the knife is unsheathed, it is a danger to you and others who might accidently touch the sharp edge. Leaving a knife out also is bad for the blade and can end up dulling the edge far sooner than if the knife is in its sheath. It is also better to have your blade in your sheath if you are moving around. Tripping and falling with a sharp blade in your hand can be very dangerous.

Also, placing a knife in the ground blade-first, as seen on many television shows and movies, is not a good idea. This always shows me the person using the knife has no regard for their knife. Thrusting a knife in the ground may look cool and keep the blade from hurting anyone, but it's the fastest way to dull and ruin your knife's edge. My aim is always to make sure the knife is in the best shape to work for me.

Don't use knives if you are mentally or physically fatigued. If your hand gets tired or blistered from using the knife, it is a good time to stop for the day. Fatigued limbs become unsteady and can lead to injury. Mental fatigue can lead to shortcuts like placing the piece you are cutting on your leg to steady it or cutting toward the body if you aren't focused. It may sound obvious, but I have seen many grown adults do this when they are tired and sometimes the consequences have been serious.

B: HOW TO USE A KNIFE

There are a few different ways to hold a knife, but I am going to focus on the two you'll use the most in basic bushcraft and survival scenarios.

The forehand knife grip. This is the main grip to use. Make a fist, and grasp your knife firmly in the fist. Make sure your thumb is wrapped around your fingers and isn't positioned on the back of the knife. This grip can be used for most cutting and whittling. As you work, make sure you try to take off only a small amount of material at a time, as this will enable you to have more control of the blade and ensure the knife doesn't get stuck in the wood.

The thumb lever grip. This grip will allow you to make deeper cuts with more control. This is good for creating notches or shaving a stick into a sharp point. Grip the piece of wood you're working on with the hand that isn't holding the blade (let's say it's your left hand). Place the thumb of the left hand on the knife handle in the V of the right hand that is holding the knife. Use your right hand to guide the placement of the knife into the wood. Angle the blade more deeply into the wood, and push the handle down with the left thumb.

PASSING A KNIFE

If you are sharing a knife, there is a proper way to pass the knife to avoid injury to yourself and the recipient. Grip the knife by the back of the blade, and pass it to the person handle first. This ensures that if either person makes a sudden, unexpected move, the sharp edge of the blade is safely out of the way.

I have often been asked about the advantages of carrying a multitool with a saw edge over a strong, simple bushcraft knife that has a fixed blade. Although I used to be an advocate of the multitool, I prefer a fixed blade knife now. Most tools on a multitool are good for helping in non-emergency situations, where you need to use a blade rarely but will use the screwdriver, can opener, and file often. They are great for emergency repairs on a camping trip or in farm life. However, the blades on these knives tend to be of lesser quality, and in a survival scenario

you'll need a reliable blade more so than the other handy tools. If in doubt, bring both, because *something* is better than *nothing*. But if you have to choose one, a bushcraft blade is the better option. Keeping in mind that you may need to process wood for your shelter; I am including a section on safe batoning, a method where you can use a fixed blade to process wood.

BATONING

Batoning is the technique of cutting or splitting wood by using a baton-sized stick or mallet to repeatedly strike the spine of a sturdy knife or blade in order to drive it through wood. To perform batoning, hold the knife in your non-dominant hand, and place the knife on the wood where you want to create a split. Grab a heavy, sturdy stick in your dominant hand and use it to strike the back of the blade sharply to cut into the piece of wood you want split. This technique can be used to split thin trees for shelter cross beams, chop wood for the fire, or cut notches in sticks you are whittling.

AN IMPORTANT PIECE OF ADVICE

Finally, never attempt to catch a falling knife. You may accidentally catch the blade and squeeze harder than intended, or the blade may slice through your hand on the way down. If you drop your blade, simply move all limbs and feet out of the way, and pick up the knife safely once it has hit the ground.

C: STUCK WITHOUT A BLADE?

If you don't have a blade, I recommend creating a sharp-edged tool in order to improve your situation. This tool will assist with most of your other needs. Stone edges are the most effective primitive blades, and the art of creating tools out of stone is called *knapping*. This skill requires an understanding of the composition of rocks and a high level of technical skill that comes with many hours of practice. I don't want this to put you off trying to create blades out of rocks, though, because you aren't trying to create something pretty. You need something practical. Certain rocks will create a usable edge simply by smashing one rock against another and shattering. The rocks that work best are usually:

- **Fine-grained or non-grained**
- **Somewhat brittle**
- **Uniform in texture and structure**
- **Lacking flaws**

A single-sided edge won't be as sharp as a double edge. But with a little practice, you can create a durable edge that will be able to cut cordage (rope) or slice open an animal. And you can sharpen your blade's edge by rubbing it on coarse- to fine-grained flat rocks.

Don't limit your thinking to metal or stone for a blade edge. Other materials that can work well are:

- **Shells**
- **Sharp teeth**
- **Fire-hardened wood**
- **Bone**

D: KNIFE ACTIVITIES

OUTSIDE THE BOX

EQUIPMENT REQUIRED:

- **Natural resources**
- **A piece of twine or thin cord**

Aim: Find five natural items that could be used as cutting tools.

Explore your outdoor environment and see if you can find five items that can be used as cutting tools, keeping in mind the list of potential natural items in the previous section. Use the sharp edge to see if you can cut the piece of cord, remembering to cut away from your body, not toward it.

STONE AGE

EQUIPMENT REQUIRED:

- **Finely grained rocks about the size of your hand**
- **A thin piece of cord or rope**
- **Safety glasses**
- **Gloves**

Aim: Make your own sharp edge out of a rock.

Making sure you protect your eyes and the people around you, smash a hand sized rock with fine grains against another rock that is as hard or harder than the rock you have. Try to hit the edge of the rock so that a small flake can break off. This will take a little practice to find the right technique, but you should be able to flake off some pieces that have a relatively hard edge. Test the edge of the rock on the cord to see if it will cut. The thinner the edge you can create, the sharper it should be. Think about your rock in terms of tools and weapons. Would the flake you smashed off be good for an axe or a spearhead?

This is the most basic form of knapping—the art of making tools from rocks.

PITCH GLUE

EQUIPMENT REQUIRED:

- **Tree sap. Pine works the best (or grass tree in Australia) but get creative and try any sap that you can find.**
- **Dry poo from a grass eater. Think rabbit, horse, or cow. Any animal that only eats vegetation works.**
- **Charcoal**
- **Fire or heat**

Aim: Make a solid glue that can be used to attach spearheads, knives, or axe heads to a wooden handle.

Crush the charcoal and dry poop into powder. Melt the sap until it is runny by the fire or on the fire, depending on whether you have an old pot to melt it in or not. Mix in the powdered charcoal and poo and then roll the glue around the end of a stick as it cools. You will end up with a ball of glue that you can simply heat up and apply where needed.

A BASIC BLADE

EQUIPMENT REQUIRED:

- **Small flake of stone that is blunt on one side and an edge on the other.**
- **Stick about 10" long and thicker than your thumb. Works best with green live wood rather than dead wood.**
- **Knife**
- **Pitch glue**
- **Twine**
- **Heat source**

Aim: Make a primitive knife.

Using the knife, split the stick down about 2 inches on one end using the baton technique. Slide your flake into the split with the thick end closest to the stick and the thinner end furthest away. Heat up your pitch glue and apply thickly around the stick and flake where they attach. I like to use a small twig to apply the pitch. Finish by wrapping the twine around the flake and stick to help keep the blade in place. Primitive cultures would do this with wet sinew (animal tendons) as when the sinew dries, it tightens by itself, but twine works as well.

You can also use this technique with larger resources to craft an axe or attach a spearhead to the end of a stick.

WHITTLE AWAY

EQUIPMENT REQUIRED:

- **A sharp bushcraft knife**
- **A stick**

Aim: Practice good knife handling technique.

Get used to using your bushcraft knife. First, remove the outer bark from your stick of choice, then whittle the end of the stick to a sharp point. Keep in mind your blood triangle, your blood circle, and your body and hand positions.

WOODEN PEGS

EQUIPMENT REQUIRED:

- **1 bushcraft knife**
- **Suitable sticks**

Aim: Carve four wooden tent pegs.

With adult supervision if required, use your sharp bushcraft knife to carve sticks you have found in the outdoors into pegs. These can be used to help pin the sides of your tarp down if you are missing tent pegs.

Find a stick as thick as your thumb, with a branch that juts away from the main stick. Carefully cut around the stick below the branch and break it off, leaving a flat surface for the top of the peg. Trim the jutting-out branch to about an inch long so that it acts as the catcher for the rope. You will want your tent peg to be about a foot long, so leave a foot in length and then sharpen below that to a point. You should now have the perfect natural peg.

E: SURVIVAL MYTHS ABOUT KNIVES

1. **Dull knives will ensure you won't cut yourself.** With enough force behind it, even a dull knife has the potential to slice into human flesh. A dull knife is more likely to slip off the object you are trying to carve into. Using a dull knife also requires more force behind each slice to make the cut effective, and if this force slips, the blade is harder to control. Fewer accidents happen with a sharp blade, so make sure you look after your knife and keep the blade in good condition.

2. **You need to be an expert to make a blade.** The art of knapping is a tricky skill to learn if you're trying to make bi-face artifacts of museum quality. *Bi-face* means that the blade is worked from both sides to make a thin V-shaped edge. I know a lot of survivalists who won't even try to make a blade, because they get intimidated by the idea it has to be perfect to work. Anyone who has smacked a couple of river rocks together will know you can get a relatively sharp edge easily. The main difference is a bi-faced, flint-knapped blade will be sharper and stronger and potentially last longer. But any sharp edge is better than no sharp edge, so just give it a go.

6

SHELTER

A: LESSONS FROM THE PAST:

On February 6, 2004, pro ice hockey player Eric LeMarque decided to head out of bounds on a snow slope in the Sierra Nevada Mountains to do a final run with his snowboard. He had seen the ski patrollers shutting down that side of the mountain but decided he was up for one more run. Fog came in and confused his sense of direction, and Eric took a wrong turn. Before he knew it, he was lost on the mountain and nightfall was coming. Temperatures plummeted to -6°F (-21°C). Eric only had the clothes on his back and some bubblegum in his pocket.

Fighting snow as deep as fifteen feet, Eric dug a crude snow cave shelter in a root well at the base of a pine tree. He lined the snow cave with pine boughs and curled on top of them to try to get through the night. Despite the sub-zero temperatures, Eric managed to survive eight days until he was rescued, continually hiking throughout the day and digging snow caves to sleep in at night. His knowledge of the best possible shelter to build in this snowy environment saved his life.

B: WHY SHELTER IS IMPORTANT

Extreme temperatures can kill you faster than dehydration or starvation. Remember the Rule of 3s? Three hours in extreme cold can be enough to end a life. The night temperature does not need to drop below freezing to be deadly. Even a seemingly warm night with a bit of rain and a fresh breeze can potentially lead to hypothermia (where your body temperature lowers and begins to affect your mental and physical capacity). My worst bouts of hypothermia were in the tropical Amazon jungle on a windy, rainy night where the air temperature didn't drop below 59°F (15°C).

A shelter will also prevent excess exposure to heat by providing relief from the sweltering sun.

If you can't get a fire going on the first day of your survival scenario, make sure you have a shelter constructed before it gets dark.

Your body can lose heat to the environment in five different ways:

1. **EVAPORATION.** This happens when the skin has expelled moisture, such as sweat, and the moisture evaporates, causing a cooling of the skin's surface. This usually happens in hot climates, but working up a sweat in a cold climate can result in hypothermia if skin is not covered up and dried off quickly.
2. **CONVECTION.** This happens with heat loss by air or water moving across the skin's surface. This includes exposure to one or more of the following: cold air, rain, and wind.
3. **CONDUCTION.** This happens when heat loss occurs by direct contact with an object. Heat exits the warmer object to equalize the temperatures between the two objects. This can occur when sitting or lying on cold ground or up against cold rocks.
4. **RADIATION.** This happens when your body temperature is higher than your environment—your body heat will exit your exposed skin to warm your environment. Your head, neck, wrists, and ankles contribute up to 60 percent of a loss of body heat, due to increased blood flow to those places

compared to other areas of the body, so it's important to try to keep them covered.

5. **RESPIRATION.** This happens when your body inhales cold air and works to warm it by heating that air before breathing it out. This results in a loss of body heat via your breath.

A good shelter will take into consideration as many of these methods of heat loss as possible and work to combat them.

C: CHOOSING YOUR SHELTER LOCATION

In survival, calories are your greatest asset. Maintaining them is the difference between life and death, so it is important to use as few of them as possible. One way people tend to waste calories is by rushing into building their shelter and making the wrong type in the wrong area. This leads to having to construct another shelter at some stage. Taking the time to explore your options before building is essential. Locations, priorities, and materials all vary, but there are some hard rules I stick to when choosing my shelter location.

Apart from trying to ensure that where you lie is going to be flat, make sure the shelter:

- **Isn't on or close to any insect nests or pathways**
- **Isn't on or close to animal pathways or homes**
- **Isn't below any tidal or flood marks**
- **Isn't located on dry creek beds (even if you can't see any rain, distant rain can still cause flooding hundreds of miles away)**
- **Isn't under any dead or heavy-looking tree branches**
- **Has the door or entrance facing away from strong winds**

As a general rule, if you are on high exposed ground, try to get lower to a less exposed location. Or, if you're on low, wet ground, try to get to higher ground. Also look for an area that has good access to water without being so close that you'll get lots of bites from insects that usually inhabit those areas.

MAKING YOUR ENVIRONMENT WORK FOR YOU

The less effort something takes for you to do, the longer you will survive in an emergency scenario. This doesn't mean being lazy with what you do, because a badly built shelter isn't really a shelter at all. This simply means wherever you can, let nature do your job. In most environments, you will find a partially ready emergency shelter already created for you. Remember that you only need to get out of the wind and rain and off the ground for a shelter to help save your life.

Some things to look out for that will make building a shelter easier:

- **Fallen trees**
- **Hollow logs**
- **Root systems**
- **Caves and overhangs**
- **Natural hollows**
- **Stone barriers**
- **Snow trenches**

These types of natural occurrences can be made into a cozy home with little effort from you. You end up only having to close gaps and add material to the roof, sides, and floor rather than building an entire shelter from scratch.

You will need to ensure a few things are okay before inhabiting your already-created shelter:

1. **Make sure the shelter doesn't already have locals.** This includes checking caves for recent animal signs and making sure any insects and spiders that share the space are friendly.
2. **Check that the shelter has sufficient air flow and ventilation.** Although we are trying to prevent wind moving through the shelter, carbon dioxide poisoning can occur if you don't allow some oxygen to circulate.

D: PROPERTIES OF A GOOD SHELTER

Creating a bad shelter is almost worse than creating no shelter at all. There is something demoralizing about making an effort to build something to protect you from the environment if it lets in the wind and rain, and you shiver through the night. A shelter will probably require daily maintenance to ensure it keeps these properties, but it's easier to do five minutes of upkeep a day than rebuild from scratch over and over.

In the Amazon, the palm leaves I used to keep my shelter waterproof in monsoon storms would wilt in days, and if I didn't put twenty fresh palms on each day, the rain would pour in. I made this maintenance part of my morning routine, and it didn't take much time at all yet ensured the roof didn't leak.

The properties of a good shelter are as follows:

1. **A flat area to lie on.** Sleep is a very important part of your mental wellbeing, so the better you can make your bedding area, the better sleep you will have.

2. **Sized to fit everyone.** Quite often people get carried away with making large shelters, but it's way easier to build a small shelter. It will also be easier to warm.

3. **No other inhabitants.** One way to ensure you don't have any "neighbors" is to clear the ground beneath your whole shelter. Insects love leaf litter, and there will tend to be more insects around if you haven't cleared the ground.

4. **Strong.** Make sure the shelter frame is solid. You will be piling layers of sticks, leaves, and other thatching material onto that frame, and you don't want it collapsing mid-build or when you sleep underneath it.

5. **Windproof.** Ensure all openings are facing away from the wind, and make sure the materials you use for the walls and roof don't blow away and are thick enough to prevent most of the wind getting in.

6. **Waterproof.** You will need far more materials than you think to keep the rain from coming in. If you can see sunlight coming in through the shelter's roof in the daytime, the rain will get in.

E: DIFFERENT TYPES OF SURVIVAL SHELTERS

There are many types of survival shelters. If something can protect you from the chill of the earth and the elements of the sky, it can be called a survival shelter. The first form of shelter is the clothes on your back, so if you have nothing else and no time to make something, try to cover your wrists, ankles, head, and neck, and sit with your back to the wind if you are in an exposed position. Anything more than this is a bonus. Keeping in mind the ways your body loses heat to the environment, pile up some leaves or grasses to get off the ground, and stuff some in your shirt and pants (making sure that it is not poisonous, prickly, or occupied). This will store heat in pockets, like a makeshift down jacket, and prevent all your heat from escaping.

This form of shelter is also great if you have to be on the move. In most circumstances I recommend you stay in the one spot and wait for rescue. But if your location is dangerous to you—for example, if there is no water around and it is very hot, or you are close to a group of predators—you may need to travel. Building a shelter every day burns precious calories, and if the weather is mild enough, your stuffed clothing and choice of location will be enough to get you through the night.

The next step on from this is what I call the "leaf box."

THE LEAF BOX

This is the simplest construction for a shelter and is a good one to know for emergencies. If it was late in the day and I suddenly found myself in need of a shelter to get through the night, I would use a leaf box.

It's quick to assemble but it is not usually that comfortable or waterproof, so don't use this construction in a long-term survival scenario. However, a leaf box will enable you to last through a night out in the wilderness. Its primary function is to get you off the ground and protect you from the wind.

A leaf box requires about eight body-length pieces of wood, along with six that are body-width. They are laid down in a crosshatch box form. Alternatively, you can do this in a ready-made hollow or ditch.

You will then need to fill the box with as much leaf litter and grass as possible, remembering that when you lie on the leaves and branches, they will squash quite flat. The idea is that you will crawl into the middle of the leaves, so you will need enough to insulate the ground and also to completely cover you to protect you from the elements. If done properly, a leaf box has the potential to keep you dry in a rain shower and warm in freezing temperatures.

One thing to be careful of is what types of critters you invite into your leaf box for the night. Some piles of leaf litter may house an ant nest, scorpions, spiders, or other creatures that will make for an uncomfortable night's sleep. Remember, at the end of the day we are looking at survival, not comfort. So the more leaves you can pile into your box, the better.

THE LEAN-TO

A lean-to is a little harder to build than a leaf box, but if done properly, it is more waterproof, more windproof, and better for a long-term survival scenario. Although a lean-to seems very open, you can fill in the ends of the lean-to to add further protection from the wind and rain. If I have a fire, I usually position it along the open edge of the lean-to, which allows me to access a full-body warmth that bounces off the back of the lean-to and adds a reflective heat.

To conserve energy, look for a place where the lean-to's frame has partly constructed itself. Examples of these include a fallen tree or a hollowed-out tree trunk. Anywhere one windproof wall is already built will cut down on the labor required. One thing to note is that rock faces do not usually make good walls, as they generally get very cold at night and suck the warmth away from your body rather than helping to keep you warm.

If you are unable to find a suitable natural frame for your shelter, you will need to find two supports, such as stumps or suitably placed crooks of a tree branch, to rest the main beam on. Make sure the main beam is long enough so you can lie down completely underneath it. Then use sticks to make struts on one side of the main branch, securing them with string or grasses where possible. Cover these sticks with whatever thatching material is available to you. This could be leaves, grasses, moss, bark, or even clay and mud. The important thing to keep in mind is that you want it to be able to withstand wind and rain.

This is also the best shelter to build for shade in extreme heat as it will allow some wind flow as well as keep you out of the sun.

THE TEPEE/HUMPY

Building a tepee is the most labor intensive of the shelters we've discussed, but it is the one I would build if I found myself in a long-term survival scenario in a colder climate.

When built properly a tepee is waterproof, tall enough to sit in, and gives you the option to have a fire inside that will keep you snug and warm on a cold night.

There are many ways to build a tepee, but the best way I know is to find three long branches (around six feet long works well) that each have a fork on the end. Prop the sticks into the ground, and intertwine the forks so that each of the three sticks is holding up the others, resulting in a structure that stands strong on its own. Place the sticks wide enough apart that you can lie down within the circle they make. Ensure the sticks are tall enough that you can sit underneath them comfortably.

The next step is to find other sticks and fill in the gaps between your three main sticks. Then cover with branches, leaves, and other natural materials, placing them over the frame you've made. Keep going until you can sit inside and not see any daylight through the walls. Make sure you leave a hole in the side to crawl in and out of.

The trick with having a fire in the structure is allowing for a breathing hole in the roof so the smoke can escape. If you are in a rainy location, you can waterproof this hole by making a cover from intertwined branches and leaves and placing it over the protruding ends of your frame so it rests above the hole.

In a space as small as a tepee, you should only require a tiny twig fire to warm the space during the night. Locate the fire at the center of the tepee and keep it small, or else you may end up burning down your shelter, destroying all your hard work.

A humpy, or whirly, is the Australian indigenous form of a tepee and tends to be similar in design but with a more rounded rooftop. I would choose to make a whirly over a tepee if I was unable to find long, solid struts for the three main supporting beams.

SNOW SHELTERS

Your clothing is going to be your first shelter from the elements in the extreme cold. Make sure you have a good layering system on if you are venturing outside in winter. The aim is that the first layer pulls the moisture from your body and helps with temperature regulation. The next layers aim to trap the warm air coming off your body to provide insulation. The outer layer should be windproof but allow for some air to get in, maybe in the form of zippers in the armpits. Many waterproof outer layers have no ventilation, and this creates too much heat when moving around that then translates to sweat. It is important to limit your sweating, as sweating is designed to help cool down the body but can have the effect of cooling your body too much, making it hard to warm up again.

Cover every piece of exposed skin that you can. If you don't have gloves or a face covering, improvise with other pieces of clothing or fabric. I have worn my spare socks on my hands when I didn't have gloves and got hit by an unexpected storm on a mountain. Try to prevent the heat from leaving your clothing by tightening any loose edges, such as sleeves and collars.

The next level of shelter in a snowy environment would be finding a natural shelter that you can improve on. Your top priorities are to be out of the wind and off the ground, so something as simple as being behind a rock, on some tree branches, or on top of your pack will keep you warmer. Don't rest by tree trunks if they have snow-laden branches, unless the lower boughs are resting on the snow line. If they are resting on the snow line, they may be hiding a perfect shelter: the tree well shelter.

TREE WELL SHELTER

This shelter is a natural hole that forms when snow accumulates around the base of a tree but not under its lowest branches or by the trunk. Dig a small entrance and climb down into the tree well. Break off branches from the opposite side of the tree or other trees to insulate the floor of your shelter, and bring in extra to cover yourself with if it is dry. This was the shelter that saved Eric LeMarque's life.

Make sure that you leave a branch sticking out of your shelter entrance to dig yourself out if snow covers the entrance, and also to be able to poke out a ventilation hole. Although it might be tempting to cover every air hole to keep the heat in, you need a place where fresh oxygen can get in so you can breathe.

SNOW SCREEN SHELTER

If you've found a natural overhang or small cave, pile up a snow wall in front of the cave opening to stop the heat from leaving and the wind from entering. I have slept in freezing conditions with a fire at the entrance to a cave and found it very cozy. But if I had to leave suddenly, I could have risked injury climbing over the fire. So, if possible, it is best to position the fire at the back of the cave. The smaller the cave or overhang, the less space you have to warm. Pile any insulating material you have on the ground. Your pack, leaves, or moss will do nicely.

Shelter may be the difference between life and death out in the elements, so make sure you take your time choosing a site and deciding what shelter is best for your location. Making the right choice the first time saves you burning the energy it takes building two shelters. Although you'd prefer to be rescued before needing to spend the night outside, it may take a day or two for rescuers to find you. Adding to your shelter every day improves your situation, so think about what it will take to make your life more comfortable out there. In all of my survival scenarios, I worked on my shelter every day to make sure it was more windproof and rainproof, and the inside was more comfortable to sleep in. Being proactive like this helped keep my spirits up as well.

F: KNOTS

Do you need a knowledge of knots in order to survive? Absolutely not. Will it help you survive? Maybe. I'm a firm believer that if you know how to tie your shoelaces, then you know enough knots to survive. I have survived for over 100 days in various locations around the world with no resources and never tied anything more complex than a reef knot—right over left, and then left over right. But the more knowledge you have out there, the easier life will be, so here are some of the knots I think will help.

The overhand knot. This is the simplest of all knots but most useful in a survival situation for tying off the top of fibers if you are making natural rope. Make a loop and pass the end through.

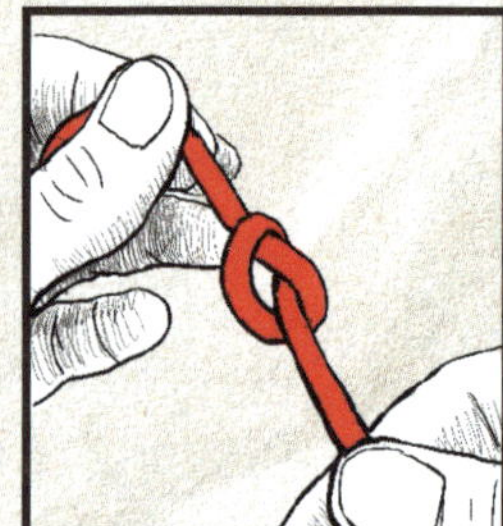

The reef knot. This is a very secure knot that is easily untied. When tying a reef knot, tie right over left and then instead of going right over left again, you go left over right. This knot is useful for tying the ends of rope or cordage together.

The Prusik knot. A Prusik is *a friction hitch or knot used to attach a loop of cord around a rope*. It will help keep your tarp tight in the wind or rain. Use a piece of cord formed into a loop. Pass the knot around the rope three times inside the loop. Make sure the turns lie neatly beside each other and pull the knot tight.

Use this knot on the top edges of your tarp where it overlaps the main support rope.

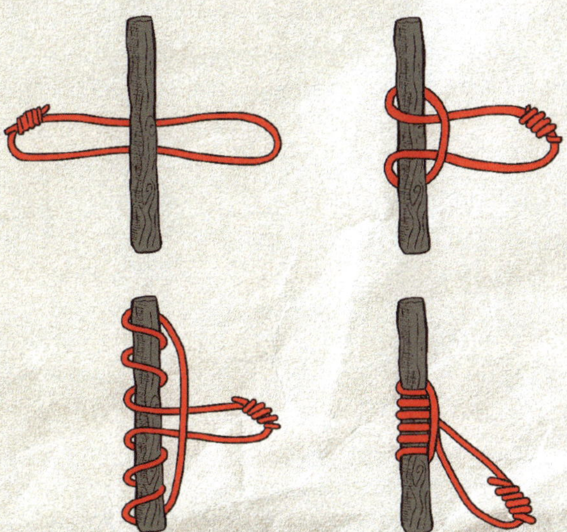

The half hitch knot. The half hitch is a valuable knot to finish off the ends of other knots to assist in making them secure. It's a simple overhand knot where the working end of a line is brought over and under the standing part.

Knots don't need to be fancy, and you don't have to know their names—they just need to work. If something needs to be made secure, no one will be judging you on your knot tying when they rescue you. Do whatever you can to make things safe and secure.

G: TARP SHELTERS

You may have come into your outdoor experience prepared for anything. In this case you may have a tarp and some rope with you. If so, then you are off to a great start, as tarp shelters require few calories to construct and are usually more effective against the wind and rain than natural-built shelters. The important thing to remember with tarp shelters is to practice putting them up *before* you need them.

SETTING UP A TARP

Hopefully you've brought a good, lightweight tarp with rivets along the edges. Ideally you will have one longer, thicker support rope, four pegs, and six smaller pieces of paracord or something similar. Tie the thicker rope between two trees or branches at a height that allows you to sit underneath. Attach the smaller rope

to each corner of the tarp and one on each side, about a quarter of the way down. Peg the end of the longer side to the ground, either straight through the eyelets or through a loop of rope attached to the eyelet with a reef knot. Lay the tarp over the supporting rope, and peg the shorter side to the ground using a loop of rope attached through the eyelet, again with the reef knot.

Use the Prusik knot on either side of the tarp attached to the supporting rope, and then attach the other end of the Prusik rope to the eyelet closest to the supporting rope and pull tight. This should leave you with a strong and stable tarp survival shelter.

There are many ways to create a shelter with a tarp, depending on what you brought. This is the only time I would recommend an A-frame style shelter, as the tarp eliminates all the disadvantages of an A-frame shape by being a solid, waterproof covering. Remember to be flexible with your thinking. And even if you end up wrapping yourself in the tarp like a burrito, you have made your situation better, so don't despair.

H: SHELTER ACTIVITIES

MARSHMALLOW MAN

EQUIPMENT REQUIRED:

- **1 bag of marshmallows**
- **1 watering can, filled with water**

Aim: Build a shelter for your marshmallow person to survive a torrential downpour, using natural materials around you.

Directions: Build the ultimate shelter for a little marshmallow person—take as long as you'd like! The marshmallow must be able to enter and exit the shelter with ease. Once you're satisfied the shelter is waterproof, it's time to put it to the test. Place the marshmallow in the center of the shelter, and let the watering can "storm" commence. You'll be surprised at how different designs work better to help keep your little marshmallow dry and how much material is actually needed to ensure the marshmallow stays safe.

LOTS OF KNOTS

EQUIPMENT REQUIRED:

- **3 pieces of rope or cord**

Aim: Tie all of the four knots mentioned in the knot-tying section in under 20 seconds.

Practice tying the knots in the following order:

- **Tie a Prusik knot around the larger piece of rope.**
- **Tie the ends of the Prusik together with a reef knot, making sure the ends of the cord are left long.**
- **Attach one of the ends to the third piece of cord using two half hitches, one using the second piece of cord and one using the third piece of cord.**
- **Finally, attach the third piece of cord back to the original rope using an overhand knot.**

Time yourself, and see if you can make this "rope circle" in under 20 seconds.

WOODEN PEGS

EQUIPMENT REQUIRED:

- **1 knife**
- **Suitable sticks**

Aim: Carve four wooden tent pegs.

With adult supervision (if required), use your bushcraft knife to carve a stick into pegs that can be used to pin the sides of your tarp down. This is a useful skill to have if you're missing tent pegs.

Find a stick as thick as your thumb with a branch that juts out away from the main stick. Carefully cut around the stick below the branch and break it off leaving a flat surface for the top of the peg. Trim the jutting out branch to about an inch long so that it acts as the catcher for the rope. You will want your tent peg to be about a foot long, so leave a foot in length and then sharpen below that to a point. You should now have the perfect natural peg. Use these to help you set up a tarp in the next activity.

A TARP FOR THE NIGHT

EQUIPMENT REQUIRED:

- **1 medium-sized tarp (10' x 10' is a good size)**
- **4 pegs (try using the ones you carved for practice)**
- **1 strong rope that can stretch between two solid objects**
- **6 two-foot lengths of paracord or similar**

Aim: Construct a shelter out of a tarp, and spend the night sleeping under it.

This is your chance to experiment with your favorite tarp design. Will you prefer a longer space at the back to sleep under or an A-frame? Lower to the ground, or a bit of overhead space? Try a few variations; your goal is for the pegs to hold and the knots to stay firm, giving the tarp a solid shape.

Sleep under the tarp for a night under the stars. Make your space as comfortable as you'd like. If you live in an area with mosquitos, you may want the added bonus of a mosquito net hooked to your main support rope and draped around you. If you want a sleeping mat for added comfort, place another tarp underneath you. Or, you can pretend you're out in the wilderness for the night and rough it straight on the ground with your bag or blanket. Make sure you bring a flashlight with you so that you can safely head back inside if you change your mind.

THE ULTIMATE FORT

"EQUIPMENT" REQUIRED:

- **An outdoor area with natural resources**

Aim: Build a strong natural survival shelter.

Scout the area to find a good location for your fort, keeping in mind the qualities of a good shelter. Use only natural materials around you to construct the fort. Make the shelter as weatherproof as you can.

Please note: Continue to ensure that the structural beams are strong and supportive as you build around them. When you're finished, there will be a lot of weight pressing down on these beams, so they need to be strong enough to support the structure.

Make this fort as luxurious as you can. Bonus points will be given for the addition of luxury items such as beds, table, and utensils.

I: SURVIVAL MYTHS ABOUT SHELTER BUILDING

1. **A-frames make good natural survival shelters.** If you don't know what an A-frame shelter is, picture a tent. It looks like that. An A-frame is usually the go-to shelter for most people to try to build in the woods, as the shape resembles a house structure, and this familiarity can make people feel safe. Unfortunately, there are a few flaws in the A-frame design, but the number-one drawback is the amount of rain and cold they let in. The reason for this is it requires a lot of extra attention paid to the peak of the roof which can be very hard to reach once the main structure is in place. This is where the rain will get in and it will be hard to escape it in the shelter. They are also hard to warm as typically you would need to have a fire at the head end or the foot end and the other end of the body will get very cold in colder climates.

2. **Shelters built of snow will be cold.** Although you'd think making a shelter out of snow would be cold, snow is an excellent insulator, as it is mainly comprised of trapped air rather

than water. This air keeps heat inside your shelter. Your body heat alone can heat up a snow cave enough to ensure you survive a night.

3. **If you can't get a fire going, you won't make it through a cold night.** When people think about a cold weather survival scenario, they often picture needing a fire to get through the night. Although a fire is a bonus and can add security as well as warmth, a well-constructed shelter with good insulation on the floor can get you through a chilly night outdoors.

WATER

A: LESSONS FROM THE PAST

In 1982, Steve Callahan's boat was sailing in the Atlantic Ocean and hit a hard object and sank. Steve managed to escape into a six-foot life raft with a sleeping bag, a few containers of food, and a spear gun. Although he was surrounded by water, none of it was drinkable. With three of his four needs taken care of, Steve's main priority was to ensure he could get enough drinking water to survive. His creativity helped him survive when he was able to make a solar still from some empty tins, a Tupperware box, and some black cloth. He distilled the salt out of the seawater to safely consume it. He spent 76 days adrift before being rescued. Some knowledge about how to create drinkable water from a salty source saved his life.

B: WHY WATER IS IMPORTANT

Water makes up about 70 percent of our body. It circulates through the blood and is responsible for transporting essential nutrients and oxygen to our organs. Water then takes the toxins and waste from those organs and moves that waste out of our

bodies in the form of sweat and urine. Basically, if you don't drink enough water, you are not getting good stuff to your organs and cells, and you aren't getting bad stuff out of your body.

How much water is enough water? Everyone has their own thoughts on this topic, and it ranges from two liters a day to six liters a day. Even scientists have trouble agreeing on this, as every person's water needs depend on height, weight, gender, propensity to sweat, and even the different ways an individual processes water.

Personally, I try to drink three liters a day, but I've survived for 21 days on less than a liter a day with no lasting adverse side effects.

Dehydration occurs when your body loses more fluids than it consumes.

Dehydration symptoms include:

- **Dry mouth**
- **Tiredness or fatigue**
- **Thirst**
- **Lack of urination (you should be peeing once every few hours)**
- **Dark-colored pee**
- **Headache**
- **Dizziness**

Next time you exhibit any of these symptoms, try drinking a big glass of water and waiting for ten minutes to see if it helps. If untreated, dehydration can progress into foggy thinking and an inability to make rational decisions and eventually seizures, brain damage, and death.

Researchers largely agree that you can live approximately three days without water, but this can change rapidly depending on your circumstances. If it's hot, you can die without water in less than a day. If you're exerting a large amount of effort and sweating a lot, you may last less than that. Even if it's cold and windy, you may be losing more moisture than you think.

Ways to prevent water loss include:

- **Making sure you don't exert yourself**
- **Keeping yourself cool (stay in the shade where possible)**
- **Not lying on hot ground**
- **Keeping talking to a minimum**
- **Trying to eat very little or not at all, as digestion requires water**

My number-one rule about water is: always carry more water than you think you'll need.

C: HOW TO FIND WATER IN THE OUTDOORS

Collect rainfall. If you happen to be in a location that does get some rain, your best bet for collecting pure, drinkable water is from the sky. Craft containers out of anything you can find. There is a lot of garbage in the world, so if you can find old water bottles or cans, cut the top off and use large leaves to funnel the water into these vessels. Get creative. Natural divots in rocks will catch water in pools, and some plants catch water at the base of their leaves. A rainstorm can be a great asset if you are prepared for it.

1. **Observe vegetation.** Vegetation cannot grow without a water source. However, some desert plants have adapted to survive with very little. If you can get to a high point, try to locate an area where the vegetation grows larger, lusher, and greener than its surroundings. This is a good indicator that water may be in that area.

2. **Digging for water.** Look for damp mud or soil patches, and dig there. Your hole might start to fill with muddy water. Allow the sediment to settle before drinking. You can also drain the water through your clothing, if you are in desperate need.

3. **Look at the landscape.** Water always flows downhill, so lower-lying areas and valleys are a good place to look if there are not obvious areas of vegetation.

4. **Observe animal tracks.** Most animals need water to survive as much as we do, and over the course of days, many will make their way to the closest water source to drink. It might take a moment to figure out which direction to travel, but following the arrow pattern of animal tracks will give you a good indication as soon as a fork in the road is discovered.

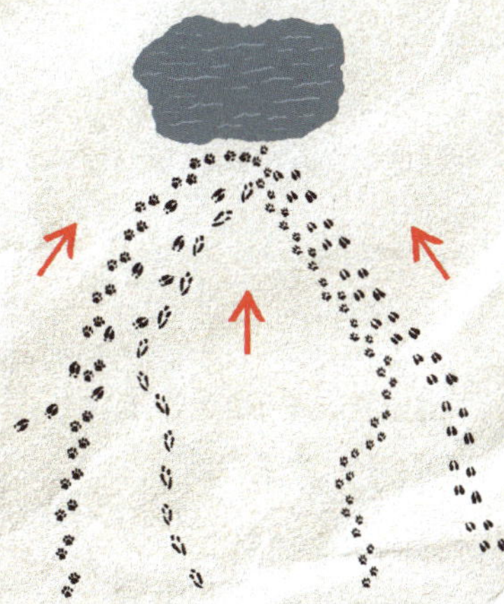

5. **Bird behavior.** A lot of seed-eating birds require a drink every day, so observing bird flight patterns can also be a good indicator of water. Smaller birds need to be closer to a water source, so finding smaller birds is a good sign water is close.

6. **Insect activity.** Bees are a great indication of water nearby, although they will travel up to two and a half miles to get it if they need to. Keeping an eye out for the direction bees and wasps are traveling may give you some idea of a direction to travel, if you are running out of water.

D: COLLECTING WATER

If there are no obvious water sources nearby, you may have to collect water by other methods. Most of these involve having a plastic bag or plastic sheet with you. If you don't have one, there may be some in the garbage around you that you can use. The following methods usually require you to be in an area with an abundance of green leafy trees or vegetation.

- **Dew collecting.** This method works well in desert conditions, where you have hot days but clear, cooler nights. Dew forms as temperatures drop and objects cool down. This forces water vapor in the air around cooling objects to condense. Water then collects on the objects. If you leave clothing outside overnight, in the morning you may be able to wring out some moisture captured in the cloth. Tying clothing around your legs and walking through grass and bushes will also transfer dew to your clothes, and you should be able to wring out enough water to keep you going for a bit.

- **Leaf condensation.** If you have a clear plastic bag of any sort, then this method is a good way to collect clean drinking water. It's a **passive collection method**, meaning you don't have to do much work to get the water. This is important, since some methods of getting water can make you sweat out more water than you get in return.

  In the early morning, place a small stone in the bottom of the plastic bag, and wrap your bag around a bunch of leaves on a

tree branch. You need to choose a branch that extends beyond the main canopy; you are looking for one that'll be in full sun during the day. Tie the top of the bag tight around the branch.

Water naturally travels from the trunk of the tree to the leaves, where it transpires into the air. Covering the leaves with the bag means this water condenses in the plastic and will collect in the bottom of the bag. You may want to swap branches and leaf bundles as the day progresses to ensure a constant supply.

- **Solar still.** This method of collecting water is effective in a survival scenario but I would only use it as a last resort, as it requires a lot of effort and can return very little water.

A solar still requires a clear plastic sheet and a container to collect the water in. Dig a hole about three feet long and a foot deep in a place that gets the most sun throughout the day. Place the container in the center of the hole, and

surround it with green leafy material. The fleshier the vegetation, the more moisture it is likely to contain. Place the plastic sheet over the hole, making sure that you seal the sides. Place a stone in the center of the sheet so that it forms a low point in the plastic over the container. The sun will cause the moisture to evaporate from the vegetation and condensate on the plastic, where it will form drops of pure, drinkable water that will slide into the waiting container.

This method can be used to distill the salt out of sea water and the impurities out of urine. It can also be used where the ground is moist, but not puddling, to draw the moisture out of wet soil.

- **Saltwater still.** There are many different and complex ways to desalinate saltwater. The basic idea is that you need to heat the saltwater so that the pure water rises from it as steam. This steam then needs to be collected and cooled in such a way that it reverts to liquid form, this time without the salt. If you have a complex array of pipes and collection pots and perhaps some duct tape, you could rig an efficient system to keep many people satisfied with drinking water indefinitely.

However, this is a lot of equipment to rely on, and you can achieve a smaller version of this with a clear water bottle and a can. You won't be able to process as much water at a time, but the method will help to keep you alive.

Cut the bottom off the water bottle and the top off the can. Fold the bottom sides of the water bottle up into itself to create a gutter to catch the desalinated water. Fill the can with saltwater, and place it inside of the water bottle. Make sure the lid is on the water bottle and place it in the full sun. The water will evaporate from the can in the heat and re-form on the inside of the water bottle, sliding down the sides to be caught in the gutter. This method takes time and sunny weather, so make sure you set this up long before dehydration sets in. If possible, make multiple setups.

E: MAKING WATER SAFE TO DRINK

If you are ever asking yourself whether you need to purify found water before you drink it, the answer is yes. 90 percent of the world's groundwater is polluted in some way, including from chemicals, bacteria, viruses, parasites, or salts. And that pollution may not be obvious. The idea of drinking clear, running water may be more appealing than drinking out of a muddy puddle, but you never know what is upstream from you. If something has died in a lovely pool and its rotting bacteria is floating down that clear water, you'll get very sick. Always purify water if you can.

This is where I need you to get flexible with your thinking. If avoiding that water will lead to your death but drinking it might save your life, *drink the water*. Just exhaust all other options first.

Most water pollutants will act as poison in your body. When your body is poisoned, it wants to get the poison out and it does so by making you vomit, sweat, and have diarrhea—all things that quickly dehydrate your body and hasten you toward death if you can't replenish your fluids. By drinking polluted water, you may feel like you're saving your life when, in fact, you're ending it faster.

It's a good idea to carry some kind of water purifier with you when you head to the outdoors. It can be as small and simple as a LifeStraw, which doesn't take up too much space in your pack and is so light you won't even know you're carrying it. Some other methods of purification that require you to carry specific equipment include:

- **Boiling.** This is the most effective way of making your water fit to drink. That's why a pot or steel cup is always in my top four items to bring into a survival scenario. If you have a fire and something to boil water in, then you can make water safe to drink. Bringing the water to a rolling boil (where the bubbles are continuously moving from the bottom of the water to the top) will kill anything that could make you sick.

- **Water filter.** There are many water filters on the market, and they are a great way of removing impurities from your water source. They usually work by using gravity or a pumping action to send water over a filter designed to remove impurities. Water filters can purify large amounts of water quickly and can last years when maintained correctly. They are a great asset to carry in your pack, as they will allow you to carry less water if you know you will come across water sources.

- **Water purification tablets.** These tablets typically contain chlorine, chlorine dioxide, or iodine. These chemicals deactivate bacteria, viruses, and parasites and make the water safe to drink. They usually require time between putting a tablet in the water and being able to drink the water. Make sure you always follow the instructions, and be aware water purified with tablets isn't necessarily good for your body to consume for long periods of time.

If you don't have any specific water-purifying equipment, there are some ways that you can make water safer to drink:

- **Straining.** The absolute minimum you should do with murky water is strain it. If your water has chunks in it, straining should also be the start of any other technique. This simply involves passing the water through some clothing so that the larger impurities are filtered out. Just remember, this method only removes chunks; it doesn't take out any poisons.

- **Seep well.** This water-straining technique simply requires digging a hole a few yards from a murky water source and allowing the ground to filter the sediment out for you. If you're staying in that location for a while, you can line the well with sticks to prevent the sides from falling in. Over time all sediment should sink to the bottom, leaving you with clear water to drink. Just remember, this is an emergency water source and probably contains impurities.

- **Straining with charcoal.** Perhaps you're unable to get a fire burning to purify your water, but you've had a fire burning nearby in the past or happen to be in an area that a bushfire has swept through. If so, you can use the fire's byproduct of charcoal to fashion a homemade water filter. Charcoal has an amazing ability to absorb toxins from water. Straining water with charcoal won't clean out all the impurities, but it's better than sucking the water straight out of the stream or puddle. Simply crush up the charcoal and layer it in the fabric you're using to strain.

  Charcoal is also a good remedy for upset stomachs and bloating. Crumble it into a powder, and mix with water. if you suspect you've consumed something that may have poisoned your system, eat it to help your body get rid of toxins.

- **Natural water filter.** In an open-ended container, place alternating layers of pebbles, sand, grass, and charcoal. The filter works best when the container tapers to a smaller end. Passing the water through the pebbles, sand, and grass will remove the sediment from the water, and the charcoal should kill any bacteria.

  The container can be created with bamboo or flexible strips of bark or old plastic water bottles, if you can find any.

- **Hot rock boiling.** If you don't have a pot, there are a few other methods to help you boil water. The one I find that works the best is the "hot rock boiling technique."

  You'll need a fire for this method, but other than that all you need is a waterproof vessel (a large bamboo stem or bark bowl works nicely) and some rocks a little smaller than your fist. Place the rocks in the fire to heat them up. If you don't have a container but have some plastic, you can also dig a pit, line it with plastic, fill the pit with water. Place the hot rocks into this pit, making sure you don't get the rocks on dry plastic.

  Be aware that river rocks have a tendency to explode, due to tiny pockets of air or water trapped inside that expand when heated. These explosions can be dangerous, with small hot shards showering in all directions.

  Once the rocks are red-hot, use two sticks to pull them out of the fire and put them in the water in your vessel. You may need to repeat this several times to get a rolling boil, but eventually the rocks will boil the water.

If your life depends upon it and you have no way to purify the water you've found, drink the clearest, most rapidly flowing water you can find.

F: WATER ACTIVITIES

LEAF BAG

EQUIPMENT REQUIRED:

- **5 clear plastic bags**
- **5 rubber bands or pieces of cord**
- **5 small pebbles**
- **Thick leafy trees**

Aim: See how much water you can collect using the plastic bag method of water collection.

On a sunny day, tie the plastic bags over large clumps of green leaves on the branches of trees in full sunlight. Place a pebble in the bottom corner of each bag, and make sure the opening to the bag is tied tightly over the branch. Leave for two hours. Come back and see how much water you've been able to collect in the five bags. This water is drinkable and delicious. Just make sure you clear any bugs out first.

NATURAL WATER FILTER

EQUIPMENT REQUIRED:

- **Empty water bottle**
- **Charcoal**
- **Sand**
- **Grass**
- **Pebbles**

Aim: Create your own natural water filter.

Cut the big end off your plastic water bottle. Place a layer of pebbles inside the water bottle, followed by a layer of grass, some sand, and some crushed-up charcoal. Pour water through the layers to see how well your water filter works.

THE BOILING PIT

EQUIPMENT REQUIRED:

- **A fire**
- **6 fist-sized rocks**
- **1 plastic garbage bag**
- **1 pair of long-handled barbecue tongs**
- **Water**

Aim: Boil water without a pot.

I would recommend adult supervision for this experiment.

Dig a hole about one foot deep and one foot round. Place the plastic bag in the hole so that it lines the hole. Fill up the hole with water. If placed correctly, the plastic bag will prevent the water from leaking out.

Light a fire. When there is a solid layer of hot coals, place the rocks into the fire. Leave for five minutes.

Roll the rocks out of the fire with a long stick. Pick up the rocks with the tongs and carefully place them in the hole, making sure you don't touch any dry parts of the plastic bag with the rock. It works best if you do this one rock at a time, so that the rocks don't cool down in between the fire and the water. The rock should sizzle as it contacts the water.

Rotate the rocks from the fire to the water until the water comes to a boil. Once the water has reached a boil, remove the rocks and wait until the water has cooled down before drinking. The boiling will have removed any bacteria, viruses, and parasites from the water, making it safe to drink.

SOLAR STILL

EQUIPMENT REQUIRED:

- **1 clear plastic sheet**
- **1 container to collect water**
- **Pebbles**
- **Green leaves**

Aim: Use the sun and vegetation to get drinkable water.

Dig a hole about three feet long and one foot deep in a place that gets the most sun throughout the day. If you can't dig a hole in your backyard, use a large plastic box to simulate the hole. Place the container in the center of the hole, and surround it with green leafy material. The fleshier the vegetation, the more moisture it is likely to contain.

Place the plastic sheet over the hole, making sure you seal the sides. Place a stone in the center of the sheet so that it forms a low point in the plastic over the container. The sun will cause the moisture to evaporate from the vegetation and condensate on the plastic, where it will form drops of pure drinkable water that will slide into the waiting container.

SALTWATER STILL

EQUIPMENT REQUIRED:

- **1 empty (16-oz.) water bottle with lid**
- **1 empty (12-oz.) drink can**
- **Saltwater**

Aim: Create drinkable water from saltwater.

The basic idea of a saltwater still is to heat the saltwater so that the pure water rises from it as steam. This steam then needs to be collected and cooled in such a way that it reverts to liquid form, this time without the salt in it.

Cut the bottom off the water bottle and the top off the can. Fold the bottom sides of the water bottle up into itself to create a gutter to catch the desalinated water. Fill the can with salt water and place it inside of the water bottle. Make sure the lid is on the water bottle and place in the full sun. The water will evaporate from the can in the heat and re-form on the inside of the water bottle, sliding down the sides to be caught in the gutter. Time how long it takes to get a few mouthfuls of drinkable water.

CREATIVE STILL

EQUIPMENT REQUIRED:

- **1 container to hold the saltwater**
- **Something to catch the steam from the saltwater and cool it**
- **Something to catch the now purified drinking water**

Aim: Invent your own saltwater still using household items.

We have discussed the method of *how* to distill saltwater. It needs to be heated somehow so that the pure water rises from it in steam form, that steam needs to be caught and cooled again to turn it back into water in a different location from the original saltwater. Get creative and see if you can make a saltwater still from the things around you.

G: SURVIVAL MYTHS ABOUT WATER

1. **It's a good idea to drink your own pee if you're dehydrated.** This theory has been made popular by many survivalists but rarely works. If you're going to drink your own pee, do it before you are dehydrated, when your pee is made mostly of water rather than toxic waste products. Usually, people resort to drinking their own pee when the situation has gotten extreme, and they're so thirsty they see no other option. By then, their urine is dark and full of toxins and bacteria the kidneys have filtered out. Introducing this toxin-filled liquid back into your system leads to you becoming *more* dehydrated and stresses your kidneys, which can cause them to shut down. This leads to you dying faster than you would have without drinking the pee.

2. **Clear running water is safe to drink.** Clear running water may look more appealing to drink that dirty puddle water, but the problem is that you never know what is upstream of you that may be polluting that clear running water. Therefore, it is always a good idea to purify water you gather outside before drinking it.

3. **You should ration your water to small sips in a survival scenario.** If you've found yourself in a situation where water is scarce, you may be inclined to begin to ration yourself to a small sip of water every now and then. While rationing is a good idea and preserving water however you can is vital, small sips are not enough to stave off the effects of dehydration. People have been found dead with gallons of water beside them; they rationed their water intake to the point their brains became incapable of good decisions, and they stopped drinking altogether. It is best to take five large gulps and use the time you have to make clear decisions about how to get to safety or how to get more water.

FIRE

A: LESSONS FROM THE PAST

On September 5, 2009, a 39-year-old Canadian named Robert Faber took a 20-foot fall in a remote area of Alaska's Denali National Park. He lost most of his gear and suffered fractures to his arm and lower spine. He tried to hike out and made it about 10 miles from the accident scene until he ran out of strength. He decided he had two choices: die in the wilderness or set a signal fire. He started a fire with some dead trees he discovered at his location.

Farber's fire was reported to the park's dispatch center. A helicopter was diverted to the smoke and saw Farber waving with one arm. He was evacuated and flown to Fairbanks by air ambulance for medical treatment. Without setting a smoky signal fire, Faber would not have been rescued. It's doubtful he would have made it through another night.

This incident shows the importance of a fire to help signal for rescue, but I've had a situation on a survival show I participated in where I needed a fire for warmth, or I would have had to quit. Although I was placed in a jungle, it was wet season. The damp and windy conditions led to me getting hypothermia in the night, even though the daytime temperatures were not that cold. It was very hard to get a fire going in the jungle in wet season, but with a few skills I'll teach you in this section, I managed to get enough of a fire burning to make sure I could keep my core warm through the stormy nights. The fire also deterred a jaguar from entering my camp, so it was successful in providing both warmth and protection!

B: WHY FIRE IS IMPORTANT

There are many reasons why fire is in the basic needs category of survival. It contributes not only to your needs by itself, but also in conjunction with most of your other basic needs in some way.

Some of the benefits of having a fire include:

- **Warmth (in exposed conditions, a fire will help you survive longer than three hours)**
- **Protection (keeping away insects and predators)**
- **Purifying water**
- **Signaling for rescue**
- **Cooking**
- **Psychological benefits**

In short, fire is one of the essentials that could make the difference between you surviving and not.

There is one thing that all animals fear: fire. With the exception of the firefighting rhinoceros in Africa, most animals will avoid the heat of a flame. In a survival situation, make it a priority to have a fire burning before the sun sets, and make sure you have enough wood stockpiled to ensure the fire is kept burning throughout the night. The fire doesn't need to be big. In most cases, simply the smell of the wood burning will be an ample deterrent to wandering animals.

There are many methods for getting a fire going in the outdoors. Almost every indigenous culture around the globe has used a different method to make fire in their region.

The key to getting a good fire going is preparation. It doesn't matter if you have fire-lighting methods on you or if you have to improvise: what you do before even making a spark, flame, or coal will be the difference between getting a roaring fire going or wasting valuable resources, energy, and time.

C: HOW TO BE SAFE WITH FIRE

As you start to experiment with making a fire, the most important thing is to *do it with adult supervision*. 25 percent of house fires are caused by young adults playing with fire. While it's important that you learn how to make and use fire, it's also important that you don't create a fire that gets out of control and causes damage to property or wilderness areas. The second you feel a fire you've created is getting out of control, call for help, whether 911 or the responsible adult in your household. Don't wait until it's too late.

When making a fire, there are a few things to be certain of:

- **Clear the area.** Make sure that you set up your blaze in an area clear of material that can catch on fire. This can be a metal fire pit or a cleared patch of ground about three feet around. Try to avoid areas of dry grass.
- **Look up.** Don't build fires under low-hanging branches.
- **Check the weather report.** Make sure there is no fire ban in place. And if it's windy outside, wait until a calmer day or try to position yourself in a place out of the wind.
- **Watch what you wear.** Wear tighter-fitting clothing that won't dangle into the flames, especially around your arms and wrists. If you have long hair, tie it back.
- **Prepare for the worst.** It's *really* important to have a water supply or fire extinguisher close by, in case your fire gets out of hand.
- **Ensure that your fire is cold before leaving the area.** Don't assume that if the fire is out, the coals are cold. Poke the coals with a stick and wave your hand above the fire pit to see if you can feel any heat. If in doubt, pour on more water. You may

have just started your fire with a spark, and a spark is all it takes to start a fire once you've gone.

D: PREPARATION FOR FIRE MAKING

The three things needed to make a fire are **oxygen**, **fuel**, and a **heat source**.

Oxygen is fortunately all around us with the air we breathe, so apart from avoiding accidentally smothering the heat source and ensuring the fire is built away from the wind, the preparation for this is minimal.

A heat source will take resources or time to make. Even if you have matches or a lighter on you, be aware that these resources are finite, so make sure you make the most of every match or strike of the lighter.

Fuel is the main thing that you need to prepare before making a heat source. I have seen many people put in a huge effort to make a friction fire coal only to have it go out while they are frantically searching around for materials to make a flame. Be aware that most methods of primitive fire making don't finish with you having a flame, they finish with you having a coal, which you then have to turn into a flame.

FUEL

Fire fuel can be broken down into three different types:

TINDER

KINDLING

FUEL

1. **Tinder.** This is any material that takes a minimal amount of heat to catch on fire. The key to good tinder is that it must be dry. Look for fine-grain fibers that can fluff up easily when rubbed between your hands. Some materials ignite well but

burn too quickly to be useful on their own. Dry cattail heads are a good example of this. They work great when combined with other materials but burn out too quickly on their own.

The best way to collect tinder for your heat source is to make a **tinder bundle** or bird nest. When a bird makes its nest, it has bigger materials on the outside to keep the structure of the nest, and on the inside it has smaller materials to protect the baby bird. In your tinder bundle the finest materials should be on the inside, and the larger material should be on the outside, ready to fuel the flame.

Good inner material should almost be the consistency of fluff or dust. Things that work great for this are:

- **Dry grasses or the inner bark of some trees rubbed between your hands**
- **Dried bracket fungus, pounded into a fine dust**
- **Palm fibers**
- **Cattail heads**
- **Dry dung from grass-eating animals, ground to a fine dust**

The outer layer of a tinder bundle should mostly be composed of fine, dry, combustible material. I find that dry grass tied into a knot, creating a nest for the smaller materials, works well. You can also use bark, palm fibers, or coconut husk.

The idea of a tinder bundle is that once you have your coal or heat source, you place it in the center of the bundle, then fold over the edges of the bundle so the coal is touching as much fuel as possible. By firmly (but not wildly) blowing into the bundle, you add enough oxygen for that coal to ignite. This is

where preparation of kindling comes in; without prior preparation, your tinder bundle will quickly burn out and you'll have to begin again.

2. **Kindling.** This is the wood used to extend the flames of the tinder bundle into a useful fire. I always think of kindling as being the size of anything from a toothpick to a thumb. Make sure this wood is also dry, as the tinder bundle flame won't burn long enough or hot enough to dry out the wood. Gather a handful of dry wood about the thickness of a toothpick. Then collect two handfuls of wood the thickness of a pencil, followed by two handfuls of wood the thickness of a thumb.

   There are many methods of setting up a fire. Some people like to dig a hole to contain the fire, and others like to make a ring of stones. I like to have a clearly defined fire area so that the fire doesn't sprawl, but that's personal choice. Just remember: if you line your fire with rocks, you need to make sure they're not river rocks. Like we talked about earlier, wet rocks or river rocks tend to explode when heated and can cause nasty injuries. To avoid this, bang the rocks together, and discard any rocks that sound hollow or are brittle. If you dig a hole for your fire, don't do it too deep or else the heat will only rise rather than spread out to the sides where you are likely to be sitting or lying.

The main things to remember are when setting up your fire are:

- **Try to find a location for your fire out of the wind.**
- **Clear the area around where you intend to make your fire.**
- **Make sure the ground isn't damp. If it is, lay down a platform made of branches to keep your fire base dry. This platform should consist of just enough branches to keep your fire base off the damp ground.**
- **Fire burns upward; it will seek its fuel above it. So leave an area at the base of your wood pile to place your tinder bundle in.**
- **Go from smaller wood to larger wood: toothpick-sized wood at the bottom of your pile where the tinder bundle will be placed, to thumb-sized wood on top.**
- **Don't pack on the wood too thick or too thin. Too much wood will smother the flame, and too little won't provide enough fuel and the flame will burn out.**

There are two main ways that people like to set up fires: the Teepee Method and the Log Cabin Method. People will endlessly debate which is better, but I suggest you try both and decide on your favorite.

The Tepee Method. This is exactly what the name suggests. Prop the toothpick-sized twigs on your cleared ground. Outside the toothpick-thick twigs, layer the pencil-thick twigs, then the thumb-sized branches. I make sure that I don't use all my kindling in the structure, so that I'll have some to feed into the fire if I have

misjudged how much of each size I'll need. Your on-fire tinder bundle is then inserted beneath the toothpick sized twigs. As the flame burns upward, it will light the toothpicks, which in turn will provide enough sustained heat to light the pencils, and so on.

If you have a ready flame, such as a match or lighter, you can skip the tinder bundle stage and head straight to making the fire. Just make sure you compensate by filling the space under the toothpick-sized twigs with some smaller, highly flammable material to get burning first.

The Log Cabin Method. Again, collect your handfuls of toothpick-sized, pencil-sized, and thumb-sized twigs. You will also need two larger pieces of wood laid out parallel to each other. On the ground, scrape out a shallow hole to place the tinder bundle into, and lay the toothpick-sized twigs across the hole, with a handful running one way and a handful running perpendicular (at right angles) to them. Next, the pencil-sized layer should sit on your two parallel logs, again crisscrossing a layer each, and finally, the same with the thumb-sized branches. With this method, you can stack your thicker fuel at the top of the cabin structure early in the fire making process, because it won't collapse in on itself and smother the fire, as can sometimes happen if you put large wood on the tepee structure too soon.

Place the tinder bundle or flame under the toothpick-sized twigs, and you should soon have a fire.

3. **Fuel.** This is the wood you use to keep your fire going. How well your fuel burns will depend on where you are and the types of wood you have access to. As a general rule,

hardwoods burn hotter and longer than softwoods and produce larger coals. These are the kind of fuels you are looking for to keep your fire going through the night. The less you have to tend your fire, the better sleep you will get.

Assuming you don't have an axe or a saw with you, the best way to break up these larger pieces of wood is by smacking them over a rock or bending them between two solid objects (boulders or large tree trunks work). If they are too large to break, you can either place them over the fire and let the fire burn each piece in half for you, or you can feed an end at a time. This allows you to burn large logs that will sustain the fire for a good length of time and also conserves the energy you may use from trying to break the wood.

Make sure you avoid the dead wood from poisonous plants, such as poison oak or the stinging tree. Smoke from burning poisonous plants can be toxic and cause death or damage to lungs and eyes.

As always, you are trying to conserve energy. Do not make a massive fire unless you're trying to signal for help. A small fire will keep you just as warm if positioned properly, and it doesn't take much of a flame to boil water.

Try to find dry standing wood or wood that is off the ground, as it will generally be a more solid wood. Any wood that has sat on the ground for a while will tend to be rotten or full of termites and will burn faster than standing wood.

Make sure to collect more fuel than you think you'll need. You don't want to wander around in the dark to get more wood if your fire has gone out and you're freezing. Find a way to store wood that will keep it dry or dry it out. I often build a small shelter near the fire that keeps my collected wood dry. I make sure the wood is off the ground and covered.

If you're trying to dry wet wood quickly, either place it around the fire or on a rack over the fire. Just make sure the wood is not so close that it catches on fire before you want it to.

E: THE FIRE MAKING POSITION

As you become more proficient with fire making, you will find your own position that's most comfortable to use as you work to make fire. The main thing to remember is that fire burns upward. It is never a good idea to be leaning over your tinder, as you don't know how quickly the materials will catch and how fast the flame will rise.

It's also important to take note of the wind direction and place your back to the wind. Not only will this help block the wind from your fire-making attempt, but if the wind does catch the flame, it will blow the heat away from you rather than toward you.

Make sure you have nothing that will dangle into the flame and catch fire. This includes loose clothing and long hair.

I like to position my body in such a way that I can quickly move out of the way if my tinder flames up suddenly. Make sure there is nothing behind you that will prevent you from moving backward.

F: THE BEST METHODS OF FIRE MAKING

I'm going to start from the very beginning of fire making and assume that you know nothing. Feel free to skip to the fire-making part that matches your skills and experience and start from there.

No matter what advancements we make in technology, primitive fire-making methods are still a good skill to know. Anything we have today that makes fire is a finite resource. This means that if you end up in an extended survival scenario, it may eventually run out. It also means that if a part breaks, it won't be replaceable in the wilderness. No matter how good modern fire-making methods are, it still pays to be good at making fire with stuff you can find around you.

There are five methods to making fire. They are:

- **Refraction**. Focusing the sun's rays into a small point to create heat.
- **Electrical**. Using a current to create a spark.
- **Chemical.** Combining different substances to create a chemical reaction that results in enough heat to make a flame.
- **Percussion**. Striking two objects together to create a spark.
- **Friction.** Moving two objects over each other rapidly to create heat.

We are going to start with the more modern and most common methods of fire making and work backward, looking first at what you might carry with you, and then ending on what you might find outdoors to help you make a fire.

ITEMS TO CARRY TO MAKE FIRE

Matches. You might laugh that I'm including *matches* in this section, but I've often come across sixteen- and seventeen-year-old students in my camps that have never struck a match before, so I think it's important. A lot of people carry matches when they go camping. And matches are great for a camping excursion, but as I explained before, they are finite. There are only so many matches in the box, and once they're gone, they're gone. Matches also are useless once they get wet. The wood becomes soggy, and the heads just crumble instead of lighting. It is always important to make sure you store your matches somewhere dry. Quite often I'll put my emergency matches into an old pill container. Some outdoor companies have created waterproof matches, but you still only have a certain number of matches and once they run out, you need to have a back-up fire making tool.

There are some tricks to making the most of your matches. First, the way you strike a match is important. Many people have the tendency to pull the match toward them along the side of the box. This can create tension on the matchstick and result in breaking the match. The best way to strike a match is *away* from you, keeping it straight along the edge of the box. As soon as you have a flame, shield it from the wind with your other hand.

Matches are a great thing to carry, because they result in a flame that's easier to light tinder with than a coal or spark. It's just important to not rely on them as your only source of fire.

Lighter. A lighter can be more reliable than matches and contain more opportunities for fire, since the average lighter generates about 3,000 flames as opposed to 25 matches in your average matchbox. The problem with lighters is that they contain moving parts and rely on a fuel source to generate flames. If the lighter gets wet, they're harder to strike and can also become rusty and can fail to work. This makes the lighter a finite resource but a better tool for your fire-making kit than matches. There are some great weatherproof lighters on the market that work well in wet and windy conditions; these are probably worth having in your pack on any outdoor expedition.

It is worth getting familiar with how lighters work. They usually have a wheel that creates a spark and a lever that allows the gas to escape from the housing and turn that spark into a flame.

Some things to be aware of when you are using a lighter are that your thumb usually needs to stay on the lever and, if the wind blows against you, that flame can get blown onto your bare flesh. The wheel can also get quite hot if you keep the flame alight for a long time so make sure it has had a chance to cool down before you spin it again or else you may get a slight burn on your thumb.

Ferro rod. This tool is often called a "flint and steel," which is not an accurate way to describe ferro rods, but is a reflection of their past. Historically, people would hit a rock called *flint* with their steel knives to create a spark. As time went by, the ferro rod was invented, combining a mixture of metal alloys into what is called *mischmetal*. When struck with a steel striker, this mischmetal ignites with a spark that burns hotter and longer than a spark caused by simply striking two natural rocks together, or a rock and a knife.

The problem with ferro rods is that many survivalists and outdoors people put one in their packs believing they're going to easily create a fire when in reality, they only have a method of getting a spark. The process needs to go one step further—to knowing how to get the hottest, most sustained spark and what material will ignite with that spark. This is where knowing how to make a good tinder bundle comes in handy.

The best way to use a ferro rod is to position the rod so that it's facing low and central to your tinder. In the hand holding the striker, brace your knuckles on the ground or your shoe, then sharply pull back the hand with the ferro rod in it. For best results, the striker should be at about a 30-degree angle to the rod. If you push the striker toward the bundle, you risk displacing your tinder before the spark reaches it.

The great thing about the ferro rod is that no matter how fast or how often you strike it, none of the gear gets hot, and so there is no danger of you getting burned. It also has no moving parts that can fail and works no matter the weather conditions.

Magnifying glass. This is a less common item for people to carry as a fire-making tool but some compasses will have one inbuilt, so it's a good idea to know how to use one. The problem with relying on a magnifying glass is that it requires the sun to be out to use it, so trying to build a fire at night or in cloudy conditions won't work.

The idea is to focus the strength of the sun into the smallest point possible. This will generate enough heat to ignite a tinder bundle. Find the position of the sun and use the magnifying glass to shine that light onto the bundle. Move the magnifying glass up and down until you can focus that light into a pinpoint on the bundle. It shouldn't take long before you see smoke at that pinpoint of light. You may need to experiment with your tinder to find the right material to create a flame.

Condy's crystals and glycerin. These crystals are Potassium permanganate, which is an oxidizing agent with disinfectant, deodorizing, and astringent properties. They usually are an odorless dark purple or almost black crystal or granular powder. When combined with glycerin, a chemical reaction takes place which produces a lot of heat and results in a flame. This is a very reliable fire-making process but requires you to carry two separate bottles and ensure that they will never spill or mix together by accident.

The reason that this can be a popular method of fire lighting is because the Condy's crystals have a variety of other uses. They can be used to treat water to make it drinkable (only use 3–4 crystals per liter), as a disinfectant for wounds, and to wash food that may have been contaminated by bad water to make it edible. This made it a valuable tool to carry, but these days there are easier and safer alternatives for these needs, so it is fading out of popularity.

ITEMS YOU MAY FIND THAT MIGHT HELP MAKE FIRE

Refraction method. Human beings have managed to pollute just about everywhere in the world with our garbage, so you can usually manage to find items that may help you make fire in quite remote locations. Some of these may work to direct the sun's rays like a magnifying glass. The most obvious is a piece of glass from such things as a broken bottle or a camera lens, but a piece of a plastic bottle will work also. I have made fire using the following items:

- **Reading glasses (if they have a magnifying lens)**
- **Clear plastic water bottle (if filled with water, you can use the base to concentrate the sun's rays into a point)**
- **Clear plastic bag full of water**

Electrical method. *Please do not attempt this without parental supervision.* This method can be a little tricky, and I'm reluctant to put it in the book. But your knowledge might help others save your life, so here it is: a charged car battery and charger cables can work to create a spark. Attach the positive side of the cable to the positive charge terminal on the battery and the negative side of the cable to the negative charge terminal on the battery. Take care to not accidentally touch the two other ends together. When you are ready with a tinder bundle, quickly touch the two charged ends together to create a spark angled into the side of your bundle.

A version of this that you can carry with you involves having some steel wool, as well as either a 9-Volt square battery or a minimum of two AA batteries. AAA batteries don't tend to produce enough volts to get the result you are looking for. Bunch up the steel wool and rub it over the two terminals on the 9-Volt battery. When the terminals both hit the same piece of wire, a circuit is created, producing energy that has nowhere to go and so creates a flame to release the energy. If you are using two batteries, you will need to rub the steel wool with a positive and negative terminal, as it won't work using the same-side charge.

Percussion method. All around the world, there are rocks that'll create a spark when hit off each other or a knife with high carbon content. The spark is generally cooler and faster-burning than one produced by a ferro rod, so it is essential to have a good, flammable tinder bundle ready. This method saved my life when I was racing *First Man Out* survivalist Ed Stafford out of a high-altitude mountain pass in China's Sichuan Province. We spent a fair amount of time above the snowline, and just below the snowline was mostly rain-soaked wood, not ideal for friction fire. I knew that pyrite was native to the area and kept my eye out for some along the thick rock piles on the edges of the mountain streams.

I was lucky enough to find some with a high-iron content and was able to get a spark into some dried and ground-up chaga fungus. This created a coal that I could make a fire out of. The weather got down to below -25°F (-32°C) that night, and I would have died had I not been able to get a fire going.

This technique was popularly known as the *flint and steel method.* This is because flint, a hard quartz, is found most places in the world and dependably produces good sparks when hit with a high-carbon-content metal. Flint tends to be a chalky-looking, fine-grained rock that is either light gray or white in color. If flint isn't readily available, most fine-grained rocks that can be broken to have a sharp edge will usually work.

If you are unsure about how to identify flint, try a variety of rocks lying around to see if one produces a spark. Even if you can't see the spark, sometimes you will smell a distinctive match smell on the rocks after striking. You have to hit the rock quite hard and sharply to get the spark, but once you get the hang of it, it's an easy and reliable fire-lighting method.

Quartz also works with a metal striker, and its white color makes it fairly easy to identify.

The only stone that I have found that will deliver a workable spark when struck off itself is iron pyrite. This is less readily found around the world, but there is evidence that some of the most primitive cultures carried with them pieces of this rock specifically to make fire with.

Friction method. There are many different forms of friction fire, but they all usually involve rapidly rubbing two pieces of wood together to create enough heat and dust to make a hot coal.

There are certain woods that work better for friction fire-making than others. Rather than having you learn each of the best friction firewoods in the world, I am going to give you a set of properties to look for that work best:

- **Dead**
- **Dry**
- **Soft lightweight wood (that isn't rotten)**
- **Sourced from faster-growing trees or weeds**
- **Straight (free from bends or knots)**

It is better if you choose a slightly softer piece of wood for your spindle (the upright, round stick) with a slightly harder piece of wood for your baseboard (the flat plank you press the spindle onto), but wood of the same density will work too.

Over the years I have made friction fires with types of wood that people have told me will not work, so try everything for yourself. One of the most important things to remember is that both bits of wood should be bone-dry. Any dampness may result in failure. Be aware of how damp the ground is where you're working. Any moisture will be absorbed into the drier wood and lead to lack of success as well.

With most of these methods, you will need a notch to keep your spindle or drill piece moving in the same place. This will be a hole for the hand drill and bow drill methods and a horizontal notch for the fire saw and fire plough methods. You will also need a catchment area for the "dust" you produce.

This dust will be the main indicator of how well your method is working. It needs to be a dark brown, almost black color. If your dust is light in color, you either need to change the pressure of the strokes or the speed of the strokes, usually increasing it rather than decreasing it. This dust is what will combust to form a coal, so make sure it doesn't blow away or fall out of the notch.

This can be a very physically demanding way to get a fire going, so start slowly with your strokes. With the right amount of pressure, you can get heat without rapid movement. As you start to see smoke, increase the pace of your strokes.

Once you have a smoking coal, take your time and transfer it to your tinder bundle. You will have created an excess of dust that will help the coal increase its size over a minute or so, which means you don't have to rush.

These are just the basics of friction fire methods. Each method has different specifics that I will outline further in the next section. If you are unsure if a wood will work, just give it a go. If the wood heats up, changes color, or produces dust or smoke, it is worth putting in a bit of effort.

The most common methods of friction fire making are:

HAND DRILL

This is the simplest of friction fire methods, given that it only needs two pieces of wood. It is also one of the hardest methods, because it requires fairly specific wood types and some good upper-body strength to be successful.

You will need a straight thin spindle (about a foot and a half long with a half-inch diameter) and a baseboard (about three-quarters of an inch thick).

Carve one end of the spindle into an arch. The arched side rests on the baseboard.

Carve a divot into the baseboard to keep the spindle in place, and place your hands flat on either side of the spindle. When you first start learning this technique, you will need to anchor the baseboard in place with your foot. Push your hands together and spin the spindle with a downward pressure to help generate the heat required. If you are creating enough friction, the baseboard will start to smoke, and you will burn a circle into the baseboard. Using a sharp edge, cut a notch into the side of the baseboard that dissects the circle, making the circle look like Pac-Man. Place a leaf or a piece of bark under the notch to catch your dust. Repeat the spinning motion until the notch fills up with black dust and begins to smoke. With enough heat and friction, this dust will ignite into a coal.

This action of burning in a hole, cutting a notch, and filling the notch with dust is consistent with both the strap drill and bow drill methods as well.

STRAP DRILL

This is one of my favorite methods of friction fire making. It is also one of the friction fire methods that requires the least amount of strength or exertion, and I have seen children as young as five years old master it. This method requires only two additional pieces of equipment from the hand drill, but it is a two-person method. So if you are alone, it's not the method for you.

You will need a piece of rope or cordage and a bearing block. I have used a shoelace for this method, so if you are wearing laced shoes then you are in luck. The cord only needs to be as long as a shoelace. The bearing block needs to have a hole or divot in it. If you are using wood, the wood needs to be of a harder wood than the spindle. You can use bone, antler, rocks, or shells for your bearing block. As long as the spindle can spin freely in the hole, and you can exert some downward pressure without it slipping off the top of the spindle, it should work.

The spindle should be thicker for the strap drill and bow drill; about the thickness of an adult thumb is a good estimate.

One end should be carved to a point and the other end carved into an arch. The pointy end goes into the bearing block, and the arched end goes onto the baseboard. The baseboard can also be a little thicker—anything up to an inch.

One person will put their foot on the baseboard and exert a downward pressure on the top of the spindle with the bearing block. The other person will wrap the cord around the spindle three or four times, then pull one side of the cord and then the other, keeping a firm pressure between their hands and allowing the friction of the cord to spin the spindle. As before, carve a divot into the baseboard, burn in the hole, and then cut your notch before putting in a big effort for the coal. Place a leaf or a piece of bark under the notch to catch your dust. The longer and smoother the strokes of the cord, the faster you will get a coal.

BOW DRILL

This is the next most efficient method of friction fire after the strap drill. The difference is that it can be done with one person, and your piece of cord needs to be stronger than for the strap drill, as it has more pressure on it through the bow. Your shoelace should still work, but certain types of natural cordage won't be strong enough to withstand the pressure.

You may need to experiment with different types to find one that works.

You will need a slightly bent stick, and you'll tie the cord to each end of the stick. I have seen people who prefer small bows, I have seen people who prefer a bow with a big bend in it, and I have seen people with very long bows. My personal preference is a stick about two feet long that is almost straight, because I can still do nice long strokes with the bow, but it is manageable and not ungainly. Your bow should be made of a rigid wood, as a flexible wood will lead to your cord slipping on the spindle.

The spindle and baseboard can be prepared as for the strap drill.

The cord needs to be fairly firm between the bow ends, as you want it to grip on to the spindle. Twist the spindle so that the cord is wrapped around it once. If the spindle wants to flip out but can be wrapped, that is a perfect tension. The spindle should be on the outside of the cord, with the arched end on the baseboard and the pointed end in the bearing block.

Place your foot on the baseboard, and anchor the inside of your left forearm to the side of your shin (assuming you are right-handed). This hand will hold the bearing block firmly in place. With your right arm, move the bow in a long, smooth motion back and forth. If you do this slowly at first, you will conserve energy as you build up heat. Once you see lots of smoke from your dust, put in a final big effort.

FIRE SAW

Bamboo is the wood of choice for a fire saw, so this will be your go-to if you're lucky enough to find bamboo in your environment. The bamboo must be dead and dry. You will need about a two-foot-long piece, ideally two inches wide.

Cut the bamboo in half. Using another piece of bamboo, scrape a handful of dry shavings off the outside of the bamboo. This will be your tinder bundle. Cut a small notch perpendicular to the sides of the bamboo on the top of one round surface. Place the bamboo face down, with the tinder bundle under this notch. Match the edge of the unscored piece with the notch, press down firmly, and saw back and forth to create friction. If you are successful, the ignited dust will fall onto the tinder bundle, and you will be able to blow it to flame.

FIRE PLOUGH

Out of all the friction fire methods, I would probably recommend this one last. I have successfully made a fire using this method a few times, but as simple as it looks, it requires a level of angle experimentation that other friction fires lack. It also requires a fair bit of stamina. But if you have no tools and can't make cordage, this is a good method to try.

For materials the fire plough method only requires a softer wood baseboard and a harder wood "plough," or you can try it with the same wood. The plough is a piece of straight wood with a flattened, sharpened end of about thirty degrees. The baseboard needs a long, straight groove in it and needs to be on a solid surface or able to be anchored down somehow. I find it's best to keep both hands on the plough and your arms straight when ploughing. Moving from the waist and pushing forward on the plough means you will have more stamina to keep going longer. Push the plough back and forth in the groove, creating dust at the far side of the groove. As darker dust forms, speed up and give it your all until the dust pile is smoking on its own.

Good preparation before you begin your fire-making method will enable you to create a sustainable fire to assist in your survival situation.

G: ACTIVITIES TO PRACTICE MAKING FIRE

With these activities I recommend you always have:

- **Adult supervision**
- **An area clear of flammable materials**
- **A good water source to extinguish the flames**

BUILD A BIRD'S NEST

"EQUIPMENT" REQUIRED:

- **Outdoor area with dry vegetation resources**

Aim: Make a tinder bundle that will take a heat source and turn it easily into a flame.

As I mentioned before, tinder is important to ensure your success with fire making, so it's important to learn how to create a tinder bundle with the resources in your environment. The first resource I look for is something to hold the shape of the bird's nest. This can be a handful of flexible dry bark or long dry grass. If it is long dry grass, I tie it into a big knot and push down the inside to create a bird nest shape. With bark, I usually just mold it into the shape of a nest.

The next layer will be dry grasses or crushed dry leaves, as much as will fit in the tinder bundle. Think of how a bird builds its nest. The bird wants stability on the outside so the baby bird doesn't fall through, and soft materials for comfort on the inside.

The final layer will be super fine materials or "dust." This can be created by rubbing dry grass together to form some fluff and catching the dusty particles to put in the very middle. Powdering dry herbivore dung (i.e. from a rabbit or cow) or dry cattail heads will also work well.

To test your tinder bundle, use either a magnifying glass or a ferro rod to provide heat, and see how well the bundle turns to a flame. Make sure you do this in a cleared area on a day without wind.

THE ONE-MATCH CHALLENGE

EQUIPMENT REQUIRED:

- **Dry kindling of different sizes**
- **1 match**
- **1 tinder bundle**

Aim: Successfully light a campfire with a single match.

Depending on your preference, you can either use the Teepee Method or the Log Cabin Method of fire setting.

Gather two big handfuls each of dry wood that's toothpick thickness, pencil thickness, and thumb thickness.

Place the tinder bundle on a dry surface where you intend to have your fire. Build one of the following fire setups around the tinder bundle:

THE TEPEE METHOD

This is exactly what the name suggests. Prop the toothpick-sized twigs on your cleared ground first. Then outside those twigs, layer the pencil-sized twigs and lastly the thumb-sized branches. As the flame burns upward, it will light the toothpicks, which in turn will provide enough sustained heat to light the pencils, and so on.

THE LOG CABIN METHOD

As well as your various sized twigs, you will need two bigger pieces of wood laid out parallel to each other. You will need to scrape out a hole to place your tinder bundle into and then lay the toothpick-sized twigs across the hole with a handful running one way and a handful running perpendicular (at right angles) to them. The next pencil-sized layer should sit on your two parallel logs, again crisscrossing a layer each and finally, the same with the thumb-sized branches.

You are allowed one match to see if you have done a good job at the setting up the campfire. If set correctly, one match or one spark of the ferro rod should be all it takes to get your fire going.

MAGNIFY THE SITUATION

EQUIPMENT REQUIRED:

- **1 magnifying glass**
- **1 tinder bundle**

Aim: Create a flame by directing sunlight into a tinder bundle.

Adult supervision is recommended for this activity.

On a sunny day, use a magnifying glass to make fire through refraction. Look at how the magnifying glass focuses the light (and, therefore the heat) into a small spot. See how the circle of

light expands and contracts when you move the magnifying glass closer and further away from the target tinder. Try to conjure smoke and then a flame from a tinder bundle. Make sure this is done in a controlled environment, with methods of extinguishing flames available. Do not leave the magnifying glass out in the sun after you're done, as it can create heat and cause a fire even without being directed by you.

SPARK IT UP

EQUIPMENT REQUIRED:

- **1 ferro rod**
- **1 tinder bundle**

Aim: Successfully ignite a pile of dry tinder with the spark from a ferro rod.

Some guidelines for using a ferro rod include:

- **Only use the ferro rod when an adult is present.**
- **Never make a spark at someone else.**
- **Never make a spark inside.**
- **Only make a spark on a designated tinder bundle in a cleared area.**
- **Always sit with your back to the wind, so that the flame will be protected or blow away from your body when lit.**
- **Sit in a kneeling or squatting position so you can move quickly if the fire flares high.**
- **Always have long hair tied back when making a ferro rod fire.**
- **Always have a method of putting out the fire handy.**

The best way to use a ferro rod is to position the rod so it is facing low and central to your tinder. Brace your knuckles of the hand holding the striker on the ground or your shoe and then pull the hand with the ferro rod in it back sharply. The striker should be at about a thirty-degree angle to the rod for best results. If you push the striker toward the bundle, you risk knocking over your tinder before the spark reaches it.

The dried head of cattail is fantastic for putting a spark into, as they catch a spark easily and flare up brightly then extinguish quickly.

GETTING ELECTRIC

EQUIPMENT REQUIRED:

- **1 9-Volt battery**
- **Steel wool**

Aim: Make a fire with a battery and steel wool.

This method of making a flame is quick and simple. Keeping your fingers on one side of the steel wool bundle, rub the battery head on the other side. When the positive and negative heads connect with one strand of steel, they will pass a current through the strand and heat it up to the point of ignition. The other pieces of steel will then enhance the heat to flame. Make sure you don't continue to hold the piece of steel wool after it flames up, and have a safe place to extinguish the flame.

MAD SCIENTIST

EQUIPMENT REQUIRED:

- **Condy's crystals (also known as *potassium permanganate*)**
- **Liquid glycerin**

Aim: Create a chemical reaction between two substances that results in a heat source.

Place a small pile of Condy's crystals on a nonflammable surface. I recommend a flat rock or an old paving brick. Pour a small amount of glycerin onto the crystals, and mix together with a stirring stick. As the glycerin comes in contact with the Condy's crystals, it oxidizes, which produces an extreme amount of heat very quickly. This heat causes the mixture to ignite and burst into flame and release smoke.

Avoid getting this mix on your skin, and always have an adult present when conducting this experiment. The best way to extinguish this mix is to let it safely burn itself out.

THE STRAP DRILL

EQUIPMENT REQUIRED:

- **A 3-foot length of paracord**
- **A baseboard of lightweight wood (1 foot long, 2–3 inches wide, and ¾ inch thick)**
- **A straight spindle of the same wood (½ foot long and the diameter of an adult thumb)**
- **A bearing block**
  - **This should be something with a hole in it that allows the spindle to move freely and doesn't react to heat. Some things that can be used are bone, antler, rocks, or shells.**
- **A flat leaf or piece of bark to catch the dust**
- **3 people**

Aim: Create a fire by friction.

This is an extremely precise experiment, so don't be discouraged if it takes some persistence to see results. Finding the right wood can be tricky, so you may have to try several different types of wood before you get a coal.

Carve one end of the spindle to a point and the other end into an arch. The pointy end goes into the bearing block, and the arched end goes onto the baseboard. Carve a divot into the baseboard, about half an inch from the edge.

One person will put their foot on the baseboard, place the arched end of the spindle into the baseboard divot, and exert a downward pressure on the top of the spindle with the bearing block. The other two people will wrap the cord around the spindle three or four times and take a position on either side of the spindle. One of the pullers will pull one side of the cord and then the other person will pull the cord toward them, keeping a firm pressure between their hands and allowing the friction of the cord to spin the spindle. It is important that the rope moves in a way that it stays low and parallel to the ground. Keep going until you see smoke and the divot is now a clean circle. This is called "burning in the hole." Cut a V-shaped notch into the circle from the edge that looks like a Pac-Man. This will be where your dust will catch.

Place the baseboard on the ground flat, with the leaf or a piece of bark under the notch to catch your dust, and resume the action. Dust should begin to gather in the notch and smoke will form. Keep going as long as you can, as smoke just means heat, not a coal. Once you can see smoke coming from the dust pile rather than the friction point between the baseboard and spindle, you can stop. The longer and smoother the strokes of the cord, the faster you will get a coal.

Take your time, letting the coal get a little bigger as it consumes the dust around it, and place the coal in the center of your pre-prepared tinder bundle. Fold the edges of your bundle around the coal, being careful not to smother it but allowing the fine tinder to come in contact with the coal. Blow firmly into the bundle to provide oxygen for the coal to grow. With a bit of practice, the tinder bundle will burst into flame.

Be careful to blow sideways into the bundle rather than from the top, and don't continue to hold the bundle if it smolders up completely or bursts into flame.

H: SURVIVAL MYTHS ABOUT FIRE

1. **Carrying a ferro rod means that you'll have fire.** The type of tinder you use to create a flame from a ferro rod spark is

more important to creating a fire and harder to master than using the ferro rod itself. Always make sure you experiment with the types of flammable materials you can find in your local environment so you know what will easily catch a flame with a spark.

2. **Using a flint and steel is the same as a ferro rod.** Both are methods of percussion fire-making, but one is using a rock type called flint, with a steel instrument to create a small, colder spark, and one is using a complex, man-made compound specially designed for fire making to produce large, hot sparks.

3. **It is a good idea to place a ring of rocks around all survival fires.** While it is a good idea to create a cleared space around your fire to prevent it from spreading out of control, placing a large wall of rocks around your fire can be bad for a few reasons. The first is that a lot of rocks contain small pockets of water within their structure and as that water heats up, it turns to gas and can explode the rock, causing hot shards to scatter around the camp. The second is the fact that a wall can act as a barrier to heat. Heat naturally wants to rise but will also radiate. It is the radiating heat that will warm you by the fire, so it is important to allow a clear space between you and the fire to get the most heat you can on a cold night.

9

FOOD

A: LESSONS FROM THE PAST

In 1860 the Burke and Wills expedition was organized by the Royal Society of Victoria in Australia. It consisted of 19 men led by Robert Burke and William Wills, with the objective of crossing Australia from Melbourne in the south to the Gulf of Carpentaria in the north, a distance of around 2,000 miles. At that time most of the inland of Australia had not been explored by non-Indigenous people and was largely unknown to the European settlers.

The expedition left Melbourne in winter. Bad weather, poor roads, and broken-down horse wagons meant the explorers made slow progress, but eventually they made it close to their destination and established a base.

The return journey was plagued by delays and monsoon rains, and when the travelers reached a midpoint camp, they found it had been abandoned by the men they left there to wait for them. Burke and Wills died around the June 30, 1861, from severe malnutrition. Altogether, seven men died, and only one man returned alive to Melbourne. An interesting point to note was that the travelers died surrounded by an abundance of native foods. It was a lack of education about the land they were traveling and a refusal to communicate with the Aboriginals in the area that ultimately led to their deaths.

B: SURVIVAL FOODS

Out of all your survival needs, food might be the most confusing one to come to terms with. There is a comfort to having three solid meals a day, and we are taught that to have any less is to be "starving." Food is the need you can last the longest without. On average, people can last up to three weeks without food. This will depend on your body type and how many calories you are burning in a day, but this concept gives you plenty of time to take care of your other needs before worrying about filling your stomach.

A healthy body can survive for some time on the reserves in its tissues, but a lack of food eventually makes good decisions increasingly difficult to make, as well as keeping warm, recovering from hard work, and fighting off infections.

You may need to change your thinking about what food is. You aren't likely to be able to make a delicious sandwich in a survival scenario, but eating certain grubs and insects may keep you alive, even if the thought of eating them is gross.

There are two different types of food groups in the wilds: flora (plants) and fauna (animals). While plants may be easier to gather since they don't run away, animals provide far more energy when eaten. Survival will quickly become a "calories in versus calories out" equation that you need to assess for yourself. If you can trap or hunt animals without burning too many calories, then the reward in energy is worth the effort. If you'll burn an excess of calories chasing down your prey, then it may be best to gather wild edible plants instead. What best suits your situation?

FLORA—PLANTS

If you can't positively identify a plant as something you can eat, *don't eat it* until you have worked through my toxin-testing steps, especially if the plant has any of the characteristics of the items on my list of what to avoid.

PLANTS TO AVOID

Time and time again, people will hold up examples of edible nutritious plants that have some of the following characteristics. I agree there are plants that fit these rules and won't kill you. However, most of the time plants on this list have the potential to make you sick or hasten you to your death. Since we need to start somewhere in a disaster scenario, I recommend you avoid consuming all plants you can't identify that fit in these categories or have these characteristics:

- **Mushrooms or fungi**
- **Milky or discolored sap**
- **Beans, bulbs, or seeds inside pods**
- **Spines, fine hairs, or thorns**
- **An almond or peachy scent**
- **Grains with pink, purple, or black spikes on them**
- **Red plants**
- **Fruit that divides into five segments**
- **Three-leaf growth patterns (i.e., three leaves on the same twig stem)**
- **Trumpet- or bell-shaped flowers**
- **Stems with leaves on opposite sides**

The next move to finding out what's edible in the plant kingdom around you is to experiment. The important thing about experimenting with eating plants is that you take your time and **do all of the toxin-testing steps**.

Beans, bulbs, seed pods:
Rosary Peas

Three leaves:
Poison Ivy

Five-segment fruit:
Jamaican Ackee

Mushrooms or fungi:
Death Cap Mushroom

Trumpet-shaped flowers:
Angel's Trumpet

Leaves on opposite sides:
Poison Sumac

THE TOXIN TEST

1. **Inspect:** Make sure the plant doesn't look rotten or moldy. Remove any insects or insect casings.
2. **Smell:** You are looking for an almond or peachy smell. If it smells like marzipan or peach, discard immediately.
3. **Skin Irritation:** Wipe the plant on the inside of your wrist, which is delicate and more likely to react to an irritant. If your skin gets red, swollen, or develops a rash, discard the plant.
4. **Lips:** Wipe the plant on the inside of your lip. If irritation occurs, wash the area thoroughly and discard the plant.
5. **Swallow:** Take a small piece of the plant, consume it, and do not eat anything else for five hours. Monitor your body reaction for nausea, vomiting, diarrhea, faintness, or excess fatigue.
6. **Eat:** Consume small amounts at first, gradually building up if there are no adverse effects.

This might seem like a long process for each plant, but these steps could save your life. I was once advised by a "survival expert" that a certain heart of palm was safe to eat. I had never heard of a heart of palm that wasn't edible, so I consumed the plant. After a few mouthfuls, my throat felt tight, and my tongue was fuzzy. I ceased eating the palm and wiped my hands on my legs to get rid of the sap. Immediately, my fingerprints became raised, and swollen patterns appeared on my legs. The sap had irritated my skin. If only I had followed my Toxin Test steps, I never would have consumed that plant and risked my life.

If you do become sick from something you've eaten, the following actions may provide you with some relief:

- **Drink lots of water, if you have some to spare**
- **Try to vomit**
- **Eat some crushed charcoal**
- **Mix some white wood ash with water to create a paste, and eat it**

The charcoal possesses properties that bind toxins to its particles and aids in elimination from the body. White wood ash can have an alkalizing effect on the stomach.

Don't limit yourself to eating certain parts of the plant. A lot of edible plants can be consumed from tip to root. Experiment with:

- **Leaves and stems (the younger, the better)**
- **Roots and tubers**
- **Nuts (before eating, boil in water until the water doesn't turn brown)**
- **Seeds and grains**
- **Flowers**
- **Fruits**
- **Inner bark (raw, boiled, or roasted)**

Although it's hard to know what flora will be growing in your specific area, there are some easily identifiable plants that are prolific around the world and are good to be on the lookout for.

COMMON EDIBLE PLANTS

Coconuts. Found on over 65 percent of the world's coastlines, coconuts are easily identifiable and hard to confuse with any other plant. Mature ripe coconuts contain a clear liquid that is good to drink, and the flesh of the coconut can be consumed both from the green coconuts and the dried brown nut. Rather than climbing the tree, see if you can find a long, forked stick to knock the coconuts to the ground.

Palms. Heart of palm is the edible inner bark found in the top of the tree, between where the oldest leaves begin and the youngest leaves end. The indicator is the trunk is usually a darker brown color, and there is a clearly defined line between there and a lighter green area where the leaves begin. Cut this area off with a knife or sharp rock, and peel off the outer layers. The super-soft white part in the center is the edible part. Make sure to run through the toxin testing steps first to see if that palm is edible for you.

Bamboo. Easily recognizable, as most species look similar, bamboo stalks are long, straight, jointed and hollow, often growing in thick stands. You can consume the young shoots found at the base of the plant. Cut them off at the base, and peel away the outer layers to expose the white inner flesh. While it's okay to eat bamboo shoots raw for a little while, it is best to boil or roast them if possible, as the raw bamboo contains traces of cyanide that can eventually lead to weakness, confusion, loss of consciousness, and death.

Stinging Nettles. This is one of those plants that goes against my rule of thumb about what to avoid. Stinging nettles are found alongside most rivers and creeks in temperate climates all over the world. They have small hairs that act as an irritant if they come in contact with skin, but these hairs are easily neutralized by scraping or boiling. Nettles are one of the most nutritious wild edibles, containing more iron than spinach and high levels of calcium, fiber, and vitamin C. It will be hard to avoid getting stung in the harvesting process, but the sap of the nettle actually provides a soothing relief from the sting. It's best to harvest the nettles when they are young and not flowering.

Cattails. This plant can be found in wetlands all over the world. The green seed head can be consumed raw but is best boiled and eaten like corn on the cob. When the seed head is pollinating, collect the pollen, add water, and make into dense, nutritious cakes to cook by the fire. The young shoots can be gathered, peeled, and eaten raw or boiled. The roots can be dug up and cooked like potatoes, or dried and ground down into a flour for making flatbreads or added to stews as a nutritious thickener.

Seaweed. If you happen to find yourself by the coast, it is good to know that there are no poisonous seaweeds. There are some that may act as a slight laxative or diuretic, but none of them will result in your death when consumed. Eating a small amount and increasing the serving over time will show you which ones may have this effect. It's best to eat seaweeds fresh rather than if they have been lying on the beach for a while. Consume them quickly or dry them for future use when you pick them, as their composition changes quite rapidly once harvested.

As always there are exceptions to every rule of thumb in survival, so if you are 100 percent certain of your plant identification and you know something is edible even if it goes against the advice of my general rules of what not to eat, then eat it.

FAUNA—ANIMALS

As a general rule, the flesh of all land mammals is edible (koalas are an exception to this rule but only of concern in Australia). This means if you can catch it and kill it, you don't have to be worried about knowing exactly what it is or subjecting it to any toxin tests.

I like to divide the animals around me into two simple groups: predators and prey. This is a risk versus reward calculation. If something is likely to kill me, it's the predator and I'm the prey. These animals feature as a high risk compared to reward. If I can kill it without much danger to myself, then it is low risk, high reward. Once I have distinguished between my predators and prey, I can then look at what animal food sources I have around me.

Keep in mind that in a lot of countries, killing certain animals is illegal either year-round or parts of the year without a permit. Trapping and snaring animals is also illegal in some countries, as it is an indiscriminate form of hunting. This means you can't choose the animal your trap will catch. Know the local laws surrounding hunting and trapping. But remember that in a survival situation, these laws don't apply if you have broken any of them in order to save your life.

EDUCATE YOURSELF

The worst thing you can do when hunting in a survival situation is to throw yourself into the situation without educating yourself. You risk scaring away your viable food sources (perhaps for good) and also wasting valuable time and energy on failed hunts.

Moving silently and slowly through your surroundings, listening for sounds, following game trails, and checking out prints by water sources provide you valuable information about what animals may be in the area. Animals tend to be creatures of habit and will often frequent the same watering holes, feeding areas, and bedding-down areas. This will enable you to learn how best to make a kill or what traps to set.

The information you are trying to gather will include:

- **What animals are in your area (size of groups and type)**
- **Where they drink**
- **Where they eat**
- **Where they hang out during the day**
- **The paths they follow**
- **How aggressive they are**
- **Their strengths and weaknesses**

Most mammals move at first and last light, choosing to bed down in the heat of the day.

Signs that will help you find the animals in your area include:

Tracks. Pay careful attention to the ground around you. Mud by watering holes usually gives a clear indication of what is drinking there. Animals like to move through the brush the same way as humans do—on unobstructed paths and walkways. They will often follow the same path, leaving clear trails for you to follow. Depending on the weather and soil type, you can get a sense for when an animal last traveled that path. Things to be aware of are:

- ***When it last rained.* Pay attention to whether the track has raindrop marks evident on it or if that track was made since the last rain.**

- ***How windy it is.*** **If the soil is loose or sandy, the wind will soon erase all signs. So a track could have been made very recently if it's obvious in the sand.**
- ***If the track is dry or wet.*** **An animal exiting water recently will leave a wet track.**

To start to understand the time frame of tracks in your area and weather conditions, place an obvious footprint of your own in the ground and observe what happens to it over time.

Droppings. Animal poop can reveal some of the most valuable information about the creatures in the area. Don't be squeamish. You will have to get in there and have a good look around to find out the information you need. Droppings can tell you:

- ***The animal type.*** **This helps if you know what types of animals leave what type of droppings.**
- ***What they eat.*** **Is there hair in the droppings, suggesting carnivore or omnivore? Or is the animal mainly vegetarian, with only traces of grass and leaves in the scat? This information can also help you know what to bait traps with.**
- ***The size of animal.*** **The larger the animal, the bigger the poo pile.**
- ***When they were around.*** **If the droppings are fresh, they'll have a coat of moisture or slime on them. After an hour or so, droppings can still be wet but not as recent (flies are usually buzzing around the droppings at this stage). Dry droppings are usually a day or so old, depending on your environment.**

Other signs. Some animals make it obvious they've passed by. This includes destruction to the vegetation from feeding or rubbing against. Clawed climbing animals will leave holes and claw marks on the tree trunk. Pigs and deer will wallow and "root" around in the grass and mud, leaving dig marks with obvious hoof prints in them. Burrowing animals will test the ground for new digs, leaving scrapings with paw marks in them, as well as their obvious burrow homes. Animals may also be digging for food such as termites and ant nests. Grubs burrow into tree trunks and branches, leaving perfectly round holes as a clue to their whereabouts. Any signs of disturbance that aren't from your habitation may be a clue to what you could eat.

KEEP YOUR OPTIONS OPEN

Mammals tend to be the obvious food of choice in a survival situation, since most people are used to eating them. But there are all sorts of animals that will keep you alive out there:

REPTILES

Lizards can be a great food source, but you may need to be quick to catch them. When preparing lizards to eat, slice them from anus upward, and remove the guts before cooking. You can place the whole reptile on the coals, cut into pieces and thread on a stick to make a kebab, or cut into chunks and boil for a nutritious soup. Sometimes you will have the added bonus of eggs, which are usually creamy and delicious cooked on a hot rock or boiled. Smaller lizards can go straight on the fire or kebab-style on sticks and don't require gutting before consumption if you cook them well.

Turtles and tortoises are generally easier to catch than other reptiles and are not venomous, but in my experience, there isn't a lot of meat on land turtles. They tend to be mostly hollow under the shell. But if the turtle has good chunky legs and a long fleshy neck, then it will be worth your while. The shells will make valuable pots you can use to catch water in or store items.

Most frogs are edible and are easy to catch once you get the hang of it. Some people like the "grabbing by hand" method of catching, but other people prefer to use a thin spear with multiple prongs on the end as their frogging weapon of choice. While there is not much meat on a frog, their legs are a delicacy in some countries. If you get good at frogging, you'll be able to provide a decent meal for yourself. They are best hunted at night, which is harder if you don't have a light source. But frogs will also be prevalent during and after rains, so if you're in a swampy or tropical region, it's worth venturing out from your shelter to take a look. Some toads can be eaten, but they usually secrete a toxin from their skins, so it's best to avoid them.

If you're unsure if what you have is a toad or a frog, the main way to tell them apart is that frogs have long legs in relation to their body and tend to jump, whereas toads have shorter legs and prefer to crawl around. Frogs also have smooth back skin, whereas toads' backs are lumpy. However, there are exceptions to this rule so if in doubt, don't eat it. **Avoid brightly colored frogs, as they can be extremely poisonous.**

Snakes can be eaten, but it's tricky to know the difference between venomous and non-venomous snakes, so snakes fall into the "risk versus reward" category. No meal is worth dying for.

BIRDS

If you can manage to find a nesting site for birds or a place where flocks gather, you can be assured of a good meal. Bird flocks can be hard to sneak up on because there are so many eyes watching for predators, but if you can figure out a pattern of where they roost or hang out during the day, you can make your way to the area before they get there and set up a "hide." A hide is merely a place of camouflage where you can sit and your prey can't tell that you're there. If you build a hide, try to build it when the birds aren't in the area, then give the birds a few days to get used to the hide before you use it. I find that throwing a heavy stick into a flock of birds is the best way to hunt them in a primitive setting. If the stick is weighted heavier on one end, it will spin into the flock and have a greater chance of hitting one and either injuring it or killing it.

If I want to preserve the feathers for further use (they can greatly contribute to warmth and comfort), I generally skin the bird as I would any mammal, separating the outer skin from the meat with a sharp blade. The skin comes off with the feathers still attached, which makes collecting them much more manageable, and you can gut and cook the bird over an open fire. You can also pluck the bird, gut it, and cook it. Remember, everything can be an asset to you in a survival situation, so don't throw away the feathers.

If you can find a nesting area, don't forget to check for eggs. They can be consumed raw or cooked. Don't take all the eggs. Leave some to hatch, in case your survival scenario stretches into the long-term.

INSECTS

80 percent of the world's population eat insects on a regular basis. Helpfully, they are a replenishable source of protein. If you can get your mind around using insects as a food source, they can help you get out of your survival situation alive.

As a general rule, there are some insects to avoid. They include:

- **Caterpillars**
- **Grubs found on the underside of leaves**
- **Insects feeding on carrion or dung**
- **Brightly-colored insects of any type**

Some of my go-to insects include:

1. **Grasshoppers, locusts, crickets, and cicadas.** These can be eaten whole, but I usually pull off the head (the guts come out with it) and thread the bodies on a small twig to roast over the fire. The easiest way to catch these critters is to swat them from a distance with a leafy branch. This stuns them and makes them much easier to catch. Be aware that if you have an allergy to shellfish, you may also have an allergy to crickets, grasshoppers, and cockroaches, so eat with care.

2. **Grubs.** These can range from small firefly larvae in the Amazon to the large wood moth larvae found in most parts of Australia. As awful as they sound to eat, grubs are a classic case of "you are what you eat." If the grubs are located inside nuts or still-living trees and roots, they tend to have a nutty flavor when eaten raw and kind of taste like buttery nut popcorn when eaten cooked. If the grubs are in rotten logs or dirt, they will have a woodier flavor. No matter how they taste, grubs are amazingly high in protein and a good source of fat, which can be hard to come by in a survival situation. The best way to figure out if a grub is in a tree or nut is to look for a hole. If there is one hole, the grub is generally still in

there. If there are two close together, then the grub has probably hatched and left the branch. Breaking open rotten logs is also a good way to locate them.

3. **Termites.** Usually found in mounds on the ground, in trees, or in dead wood, termites can be harvested by breaking off a chunk of the mound and shaking them free. Eat them raw or roast them in a pan. You can also eat their larvae. If you find a dead branch with termites living in it, you can put one end of the branch on the fire and catch them as they retreat from the heat. Termites are also useful for a variety of other tasks. They can help you find north, as they tend to make their nests on the sunniest side of the tree. This is the north in the Southern Hemisphere and the south in the Northern Hemisphere. Regardless of the specifics, you can make sure that you're not going around in circles simply by making sure you keep the termite nests consistently on one side the direction you are traveling. Crushing termites between your hands and rubbing them on your exposed skin can help deter insects, and wetting down the termite nest itself will provide you with a sticky clay that is great for making pots and bowls.

4. **Mollusks.** In the ocean mollusks usually can be located between the high- and low-tide mark on rocks or under the beach sand, where holes or divots will give them away. Dig a foot down into the wet sand, where you see those clues. You may need a sharp edge to pry them off the rocks, or just smash the outer shell and scoop out with a sharpened twig. Avoid any mollusks that are brightly colored, and do not eat them if the following occurs:
    - **They remain partially open when you touch them.**
    - **They are easy to remove from the rocks or have fallen off by themselves.**
    - **They smell "off."**
    - **They are located in water with a reddish-tinged algae.**

Do not eat mollusks that are bright in color or shaped like cones. One species of cone shell is one of the most venomous creatures on the planet. There are over 400 different species of cone shells and not all of them are deadly. However, most will deliver a venomous barb that ranges from extremely painful to life-threatening if it pierces your skin, so they are best avoided entirely.

My biggest recommendation with wild meats is to cook them well. Overcook them, if in doubt. Unlike store-bought meats, wild meats can contain parasites and diseases that could make you sick if consumed raw. The best way to kill these is by boiling or roasting.

C: HUNTING

Hunting can be broken down into two different types: passive and active. Passive hunting is when you put a mechanism in place and wait for the mechanism to secure the animal for you. This includes traps and snares. Active hunting is when you're pursuing an animal and kill it through force. This includes chasing it down on foot and using weapons.

PASSIVE HUNTING

The advantage of passive hunting is that you can set multiple traps and snares, increasing your chances of getting a meal. Set as many traps and snares as you can make. Then you can use your time and energy for other activities, such as collecting wood and maintaining your shelter.

As mentioned previously, traps and snares are illegal in many countries, so remember: if you are practicing traps and snares, or if you get rescued, dismantle them before you leave. If you are in a survival situation with multiple people, make sure everyone knows where the traps and snares are set so that no one gets unnecessarily injured.

SETTING TRAPS AND SNARES

Once a human has moved into an environment, most likely the

animals will move out. Your scent, movement, and fire will scream *predator* and your prey will take their family elsewhere.

When you set traps and snares, here are a few important things to keep in mind:

- **Build the traps and snares a good distance away from your shelter.**
- **Don't disturb the environment too much; it will cause some animals to avoid the area.**
- **Locate your traps and snares close to areas with signs of animals, such as burrows and game trails.**
- **Camouflage the traps and snares the best you can using natural materials.**
- **Make traps and snares strong; an animal struggling for its life will fight a lot harder than you anticipate.**
- **Bait the trap with something you know the animal eats or has been eating; their droppings will give you an idea of some of their favorite foods.**
- **Check your traps regularly; not only is it inhumane to leave an animal suffering needlessly, they also may figure out a way of escaping the trap if they have enough time.**

You'll need to be creative in your environment to figure out what traps will work for you. Look at the surrounding terrain. Do you have an abundance of rocks and hard ground? If you do, don't dig a pitfall as it will be too hard in the hard ground, but instead use a deadfall which can be set on top of that hard soil. For more on this, see pages 132–135. Do you have cord on you? If so, then snares might be your best option.

EXAMPLES OF SNARES

Snares work by trapping an animal by a body part. The rope or cord is usually set in such a way that the more the animal struggles, the tighter the cord becomes. For all my snares, I use a simple noose knot, where one end of the rope is threaded through a loop tied in the other end.

The Basic Snare. This works best where you've located some burrows or clear game trails of smaller animals. You need:

- **At least 3 feet of cord or rope**
- **2 small, forked sticks**
- **A strong anchor point**

The anchor can be the base of an existing tree or shrub, or a thick stick you bang into the ground. Make sure you put the anchor stick beside the burrow rather than behind it, as you may cause the entrance to cave in. If you're setting up on a game trail, have the anchor off to the side. Make the loop about four to five inches wide, and set it about four fingers width off the ground, using the two small, forked sticks to support it. The idea is that the head of the animal will pass into the loop, but the rest of the body won't, and as the animal moves forward, the loop will squeeze around the animal's neck. It's important to picture how the snare will work to set it properly for the type of game you are after.

If you are setting these snares by burrows, remember that an animal will usually have multiple exits to their burrow. Search around the area and set a snare on every burrow you can find.

The Tension Snare. For a quicker kill and to remove your prey from other ground predators, consider a tension snare. You will need:

- **At least 3 feet of rope**
- **A trigger stick/anchor bar setup made of 2 pieces of wood, each the width of your thumb**
- **A sapling or branch you can pull downward for tension**
- **2 small, forked sticks**

The snare part of the setup is the same used for the simple snare. The tricky part is to locate the perfect tension branch. It needs to be flexible and long enough to suspend the prey off the ground, yet also needs enough rigidity to snap back into place once triggered. It needs to be positioned by a game trail or burrow.

The trigger bar needs to be notched or forked so that it interlocks with the anchor bar. The anchor bar gets hammered into the ground, and the trigger bar is tied to roughly the middle of the rope. One end of the rope is tied around the tensioned branch, and the other end of the rope forms the snare or noose. I find it easier to take care of the tensioned branch first, setting the trigger stick and then delicately positioning the snare on the game trail or in front of the burrow, perched on the small, forked sticks. Just make sure you've threaded your noose knot first before tying the other end to the tree. Test your snare by triggering it with a stick. This will enable you to see if the trigger stick is sensitive enough and if the tension branch will work.

The Platform Snare. This can be used for bigger game, with the idea that you will catch them and hold them in place by a leg rather than their neck. The concept is similar to the tension snare. You will need:

- **3 to 5 feet of rope, depending on your target animal**
- **A branch or sapling that you can pull down for tension**
- **2 thick anchor sticks with forks**
- **2 thinner, longer sticks to aid the trigger mechanism**
- **A trigger stick**
- **Thin twigs and leaf matter to build and disguise a platform**

Hammer the two anchor sticks on either side of the game trail with the forks facing downward. Place one of the trigger aids between the two anchor sticks under the fork. The other trigger

aid will be placed near the ground on the opposite side. The trigger stick needs to be long enough to reach between the two. Make your noose and attach the trigger stick close to the noose end, with enough slack for the noose to lie on the path to one side of the snare. The other side of the rope is then attached to the branch and tensioned. The trigger stick feeds under and to one side of the top trigger aid. The bottom trigger aid is then positioned to keep the trigger stick in position. I like having my trigger stick to the side of the snare that the tensioned branch is on, so as not to deter the animal from its path.

A platform is then made with light sticks and leaves over the bottom trigger aid. Be careful not to make the platform material too heavy, or else the weight will trigger the snare. Place the noose on top of the platform.

It's a good idea to test this snare before building the platform by pressing down on the bottom trigger aid. Some common mistakes are to have the trigger aid too close to the ground to create enough movement to trigger the snare, or to have the trigger stick too long so it catches on the ground rather than freely triggers.

EXAMPLES OF TRAPS

The most common survival traps are deadfalls. As suggested by the name, these are traps that kill an animal by having something heavy fall on them. While they are usually set for smaller game, historically there are examples of larger animals, such as leopards, being killed with them. Smaller deadfalls can be set up by one person, but the larger ones will require more than one person to set up safely.

While deadfall traps have quickly become the bushcraft trap of choice, as they are fun to demonstrate and easy to set up, it is important to note that most of them are demonstrated in a way that would lead them to fail in a real-life scenario. The characteristics that contribute to their success or failure are:

- **The weight of the deadfall**
- **The density of the ground below the deadfall**
- **The speed of the trigger mechanism**

I have seen many deadfalls set up in a way where the weight would be insufficient to kill the target prey, leading to the animal being able to squeeze out from under the trap. If the ground below the deadfall is soft or uneven, this will also provide an escape route for your food. The trigger mechanism can be hesitant, and this will allow the critter time to dash out from under the deadfall once it starts to move. All of these things will be the difference between eating dinner and going hungry.

While a heavy, flat rock is ideal for a deadfall, if your prey of choice is middle to larger sized, or there are no suitable rocks available, you can strap logs together like a raft and load the top of the logs with heavy material, such as dirt or smaller rocks, in order to add some weight.

Figure 4 Deadfall. This is one of the more popular deadfall traps, due to the limited materials required to make one. You will need:

- **A heavy, flat rock or deadfall**
- **3 pieces of wood as thick as your thumb**
- **Bait**

One piece of wood is the bait stick. It needs a square notch on one side and a 7-notch at one end. One stick is the anchor stick. It needs to have a matching square notch on its side to marry to the bait stick and the top end sharpened on one side. The pivot stick then has a V-notch that marries to the top of the anchor stick and a double-sharpened end to marry into the 7-notch. The deadfall rests on the other end of the pivot stick. Sounds complicated, but it's quite simple once you have an understanding of how it goes together. The bait is placed on the short end of the bait stick under the deadfall.

Some things to be aware of are making sure that the anchor stick is located on the outside of the deadfall, otherwise the deadfall will get stuck on the anchor stick when triggered. It's also important to keep the end of the bait stick short so it doesn't get in the way of the deadfall. Practice triggering the deadfall until the trigger mechanism is sensitive and swift.

Paiute Deadfall. I find that the trigger mechanism with this deadfall trap can be a little faster than the Figure 4, but it does require some extra equipment. You need:

- **A heavy, flat rock or deadfall**
- **An anchor stick**
- **A thin trigger stick**
- **A pivot stick**
- **A toggle**
- **Some cord or rope**
- **Bait**

For a smaller version of this trap, the cord does not need to be very strong. I've used an unprocessed palm leaf in its place and it worked perfectly, so don't get hung up on needing to have or create the perfect piece of rope.

Some people like their anchor stick to have a fork in the end, but I find this has the potential to slow down the trigger mechanism. I find it works best to make a sharpened V-shape on the end of the anchor stick and have a matching V-notch in the pivot stick. Flatten one end of the pivot stick so the deadfall sits on it more easily, and tie the rope to the other end of the pivot stick. The toggle is tied around the middle to the other end of the rope and wrapped around the anchor stick about an inch or two off the ground. I like to make my toggle flat on one side and carve a divot in it where the trigger stick sits. Bait is then placed in the middle of the trigger stick that sits under the deadfall or on the ground underneath it. The other end of the trigger stick uses the underside of the deadfall in opposition to the toggle.

Make sure the anchor stick isn't preventing the deadfall from hitting the ground by locating it outside the lip of the deadfall. While setting up, I like to prop up the deadfall with something that prevents it from crushing my hands if it accidentally triggers.

Be wary that the meat from deadfalls can be polluted by burst digestive tracts. If in doubt, do not eat the meat or wash it thoroughly and overcook it, as it can make you very sick.

The Arapuca Trap. This is a bird trap I've found to be effective when catching ravens and jays in North America. Since it's a live capture trap, they were released unharmed, but in a survival scenario, the birds would have made a good meal. The trap requires quite a bit of assembly but can be used multiple times, so it's worth the effort. You can use a variety of trigger mechanisms for this trap. **The triggers used in the Figure 4 and Paiute traps work well**, but I will add in another mechanism to expand your tool kit of trap triggers. You will need:

- **24 thumb-width sticks with 5 sets of 4 varying sizes**
- **2 pieces of rope or cord about 2 feet in length**
- **A short length of cord**
- **A finger-width trigger stick about 10 inches long**
- **Bait**

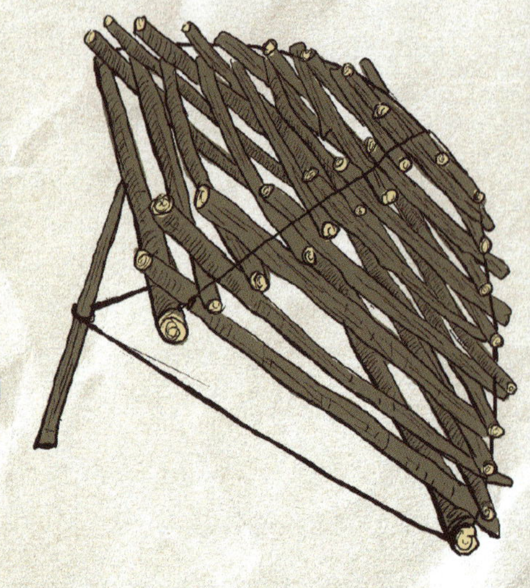

Place the two longest sticks side by side, and attach the two pieces of cord from one end of each stick to the other to create a square. Twist the two sticks once in opposite directions so the rope forms a cross. Slide the next two longest sticks, log cabin style, between the ropes and begin to fill in the slack. Eventually you will end up with a tensioned pyramid. This is your cage. You may need to fill in the top of the pyramid with sticks to ensure that there isn't an escape route for the bird. These are also the sticks you will remove to get the bird out without it escaping. Break the trigger stick in half in such a way that you can put the pieces back together again. Tie the short length of the cord to the inside of the trap, and loop it around the break in the trigger stick with tension. Lean the trap on the trigger stick. Place the bait inside the trap. When a bird enters the trap, it will disturb the cord, which will trigger the trap. I find that it is necessary to put a weight on top of the trap to make sure the bird doesn't manage to overturn the trap or wriggle out from under it.

With traps and snares, create a natural flow or path to funnel the animal into the trap, and make it hard for them to go around the trap. Do this by building up the pathway on the sides leading to the trap, or making the clearest path through the undergrowth the one that passes by the trap. This is best done with the material in the area so as not to alert the animal to anything suspicious.

Make sure you are cautious when approaching triggered traps and snares. Wild animals can be extremely vicious when trapped and injured. Approach slowly and have a backup weapon such as a knife, club, or spear in case you need to finish the job. Don't grab an animal with your bare hands until you have made sure it's dead.

A basic knowledge of the way traps and snares operate could save your life. If one trap doesn't work, try another. Even if you can't remember an exact trap, just an understanding of how traps work could be enough for you to make your own and provide yourself with food to survive.

FISHING

I place fishing between passive and active hunting because it's a little bit of both. It's passive since you can set multiple lines and wait for them to catch a fish, but it's also valuable to be actively watching and waiting for a fish to get on your line, so it's difficult to go away and work on other projects.

If you're fortunate enough to have ended up next to a body of water in your survival situation, fishing should be your best chance of getting some food. It's a good idea to learn some fishing techniques before you end up in an emergency situation. Fishing can be a fun activity to get you outdoors, and there is nothing more rewarding than eating something you've caught yourself. Some tips on how to start fishing are as follows:

Choose the right gear. The first step to successful fishing is choosing the right gear. You'll need a fishing rod, reel, line, and bait or lures. As you're starting out, it's best to get advice from someone with experience as to what rod will work best for you.

Learn how to cast. Before you can catch any fish, you'll need to learn how to cast your line. The basic casting technique involves holding the rod with both hands, pulling back the line with your dominant hand, and then flicking the rod forward to send the line out into the water. Practice casting on land first to get a feel for it before you try it on the water. If you are casting with a hand line, spool some slack next to you on a clear patch of ground and, as you throw the baited hook toward the water, aim the hand line toward the water to allow the line to freely flow. Different hand lines will require different techniques, but this method is a good place to start to see what works best with yours.

Choose the right bait or lures. The type of bait or lures you use will depend on the fish you're targeting. Some fish prefer live bait like worms, while others are attracted to lures that mimic small fish or insects. Ask someone at your local tackle shop for advice on what bait or lures work best in your area.

Be patient. Fishing requires patience and persistence. You may not catch anything on your first few tries, but don't get discouraged. Keep casting and trying different bait or lures until you find what works.

Observe your surroundings. Look for signs of fish activity like ripples on the surface of the water or jumping fish. Pay attention to the weather and how it affects the water conditions. The more you observe and learn, the better you'll become at fishing.

ATTACHING AND BAITING A HOOK

The best knot to tie to attach a hook to a line is the fisherman's knot. It's a bit tricky to explain, but hopefully the diagram will make it clear.

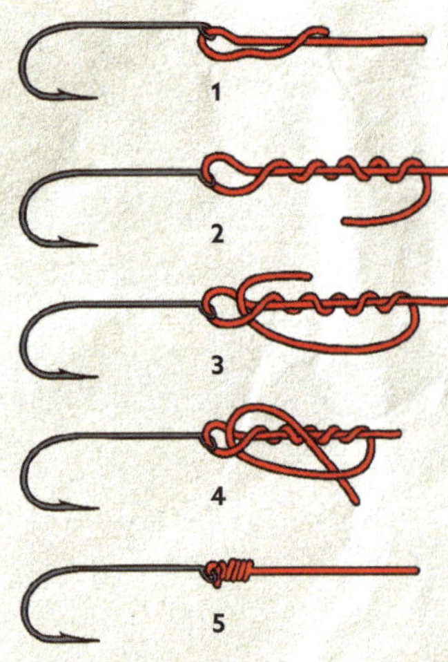

When tying this knot the important thing is to grasp the hook firmly between your pointer finger and thumb so that it doesn't catch on anything or prick your skin. Feed the end of the fishing line through the loop on the fishing hook until you have a couple of inches through. Make a bend in the piece you threaded through about halfway along, and wrap that end around the other piece of line about five times, going downward toward the hook. Once this is done, feed the end of the line up through the loops you just made, staying parallel to the main line. Once the feeder line is through, cinch the knot down onto itself and the hook, creating a strong knot to keep your hook on your line.

When baiting your hook, again, be careful not to get your fingers caught on the sharp hook, and loop the bait through the hook a few times to make sure it is secure on the hook.

Some tips to stay safe while fishing include:

- **Choose a good location**
  When choosing a location to fish, make sure it's safe and free from hazards. Look for areas with good visibility and no overhead power lines or trees. Avoid fishing near fast-moving water or in areas with steep banks or cliffs. It's also a good idea to fish with a friend, as it's always safer to have someone else around in case of an emergency.

- **Handle hooks carefully**
  Baiting hooks can be a dangerous task if not done carefully. Always handle hooks with caution, and avoid touching the pointed end. If the hook gets stuck in your skin, don't panic. Remain calm and try to carefully remove the hook. If the hook remains stuck after a few gentle attempts, seek medical attention if necessary.

- **Practice safe casting**
  Safe casting is essential for preventing accidents while fishing. Make sure to always look around you before casting, and avoid casting near other people or objects. Keep a safe distance from others, and make sure you have plenty of space to cast.

- **Wear proper attire**
  When fishing, it's important to wear appropriate clothing and gear. Wear nonslip shoes or boots with good traction, as fishing can be slippery and wet. Wear clothing that's appropriate for the weather conditions, and bring a hat and sunglasses to protect yourself from the sun. If you're fishing in cold weather, dress in layers and wear waterproof clothing. If you're fishing from a boat, make sure to wear a life jacket at all times.

- **Handle fish with care**
  For your safety and the well-being of the fish, it's important to handle the fish with care. Use a landing net to safely bring the fish to shore. Some fish have sharp or poisonous fins, so make sure that you avoid touching those areas unless you're sure of the fish type and know you won't be harmed.

ANCIENT FISHING TECHNIQUES

If you don't have hooks and nylon line, fishing might be a little trickier. But there are all kinds of ancient fishing techniques to try:

Fishing line. If you happen to have some paracord on you, then pulling the inner threads out and tying them together creates a great line.

Hooks. Primitive hooks were shaped out of bone, antler, shell, thorns, and even hardwood. Look for something you can carve or shape into a hooklike structure that can be sharpened and maintains its strength.

I have seen people have success with a small, straight, sharpened piece of wood as a hook. This works well for catfish, eels, and any type of bottom-feeder fish. Sharpen both ends of a small, strong stick the length of a toothpick, and attach it to the end of your line. Tie the bait on the stick in such a way that it holds the stick parallel to the line, but so that the stick will open out when the bait is consumed. Once the fish swallows the bait and hook, the stick lodges in its stomach.

Float. Any porous or buoyant wood will work. Tie it to your line so the hook dangles in the water rather than sits on the bottom. This will increase your chances of attracting a bite.

Bait. Get creative. Most of the best baits we purchase are gathered from nature. Worms, shellfish, grubs, crickets, innards, and even berries will work. If you're in an area with termite mounds, you can break off a chunk and shake it over your fishing area. The termites falling onto the water surface will chum the water and can create a feeding frenzy.

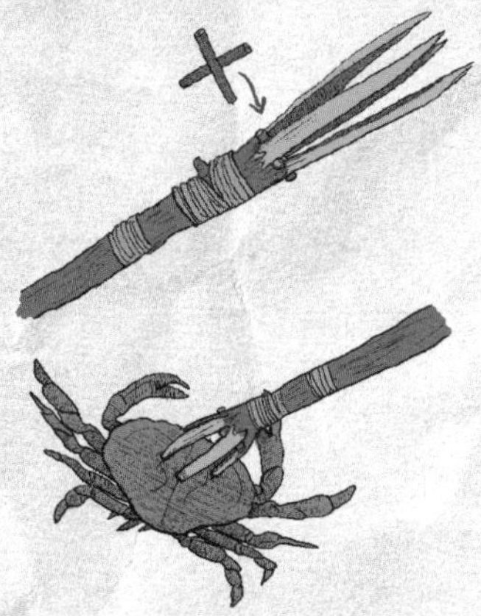

Spears. For fishing or crabbing, cut the end of a stick into four segments. Sharpen each of these segments. Tie two opposing short sticks in the middle of these four segments to create some space between them.

Traps. Some of the oldest man-made structures discovered are coastal fish traps believed to have been constructed over 60,000 years ago. If you're in a tidal area, a rock pool fish trap is a good one to consider. Create an area at low tide where a pool of water becomes isolated from the ocean water by a raised wall of rocks. At high tide, the fish will have access to the area but will become stranded in there as the water retreats. This will make them easier to spear or catch.

Fish dam. If you are by a stream, you can use a similar technique of building rock walls to trap fish. Shape a funnel of rocks across part or all of the stream that ends in a rock wall and catchment area on the downstream side.

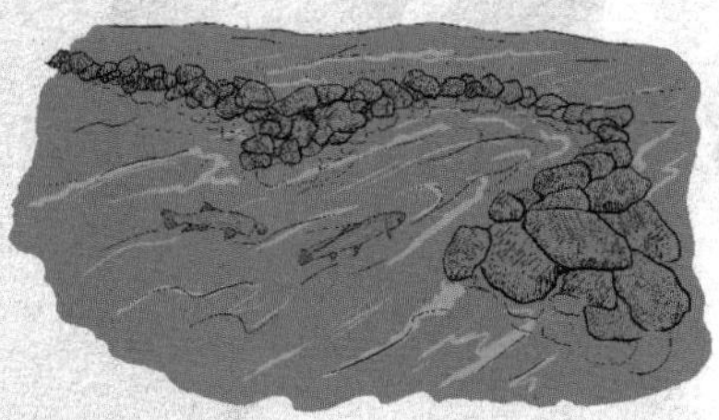

Never eat dead fish you find floating on the surface, even if it seems like easy food. Dead fish harbor bacteria, parasites, and diseases that can make you very sick. Also be wary of the water you found it in, and don't drink it if you have other choices.

It might take you some time to learn the habits of the fish in your area. Be persistent and try different methods, different times of day, and different baits.

PREPARING YOUR FISH

Properly cleaning a fish is essential for preparing it for cooking and can make a big difference in the taste and quality of your meal. Be aware that some fish have sharp spines or spikes along their fins and avoid getting cut on these.

The first step in preparing a fish for cooking is to scale it. To do this, you'll need a blunt knife or some kind of sharp edge like a rock flake or a shell. Hold the fish firmly by the tail with one hand, and use the edge to scrape the scales off in a downward motion, starting at the tail and working your way toward the head. Rinse the fish thoroughly to remove any loose scales. You can also place the fish directly on the coals to burn off the scales but make sure you don't burn the flesh as well. Some fish, like catfish, may not have scales. If they don't then proceed to the next step.

After scaling the fish, the next step is to gut it. To do this, you'll need a sharp knife and a clean surface to work on, if possible. Start by making a small incision at the base of the fish's belly, near the tail. Using the tip of the knife, carefully cut along the belly toward the head, being careful not to puncture any internal organs. Once you've reached the gills, use your fingers to remove the organs from the cavity, being sure to remove everything including the intestines, liver, and stomach. Rinse the cavity thoroughly with water.

ACTIVE HUNTING

There are a lot of things to think about when trying to get close to an animal. They include:

- ***Wind direction.*** **Is it blowing your smell to the animal or away from it?**
- ***How noisy you are.*** **Are there dead leaves underfoot or can you move quietly?**
- ***What usually hunts your prey.*** **Are they expecting attacks?**
- ***When they're not paying attention.*** **When are they most distracted from keeping an eye out for danger?**
- ***If they will see you.*** **Can you disguise yourself or remain hidden?**

It might take you a while to develop the skills necessary to get close enough to actively hunt the animals in your area.

My two favorite primitive hunting weapons are the spear and the throwing stick.

SPEAR

All you need for a basic spear is a long, strong, straight piece of wood. I prefer to cut one from a sapling, as they're easier to process while green, but any wood that fits that description will do. Sharpen one end to a point, and you have a workable spear.

THROWING STICK

The most advanced form of throwing stick is the boomerang, but you don't need to make one that comes back. Find a dense piece of wood about two feet long with a slight bend and one side heavier than the other. Throwing this boomerang so that it flies end over end can make a deadly weapon. If you have the time and the blade, you can flatten the top and bottom side to make it more aerodynamic, but it's not necessary. A throwing stick is perfect for taking out individual birds in a flock, either on the ground or on the wing. It is also great for smaller ground-dwelling animals.

CLUB

A stick with a heavier knot of wood on the end of it works perfectly for a club. This is a good weapon to finish off injured animals or as a form of defense.

D: PREPARING WILD FOOD

Once you've managed to kill an animal, you need to know how to process it to get the most food from that kill. You don't want anything useful to go to waste. Helpful hint: this should be done at a location away from your shelter so you don't attract predators to your camp.

With most animals, except the very small ones, I recommend removing the digestive tract first. If the intestines or stomach are punctured, the animal's waste will pollute your meat and can lead to you getting sick if you eat it. There are many ways to process an animal, but I like to keep it simple. Every animal is different on the inside, but my steps for processing remain the same.

1. **Skin the animal. Make a shallow cut in the hide, usually in the middle of the belly. You will find there is a distinct difference between skin and meat; they're separated by a layer of connective tissue called *fascia*. Cut between the skin and meat to remove the hide.**

2. **Find the anus of the animal, and make a shallow cut on the inner skin layer, going toward the throat until you reach the rib cage.**
3. **Remove the organs.**
4. **Cut off as much of the meat as you can see.**
5. **If the animal has horns or any other defining feature, collect that as well.**
6. **Cook the meat well, as wild meat can have parasites that'll make you sick if you eat the meat raw. I like to cook my meat either straight on the coals or threaded on a stick and cooked over the flames.**

STORING YOUR MEAT

If you have hunted more than you can eat in one sitting, you'll need to figure out a method of storing the meat. Unless your meat is sitting in full sun or has attracted flies, fresh meat can last about three days without being treated. Methods to store meat include:

Sun drying. Cut the meat into thin strips and lay across rocks or a rack of branches. You'll need to have the meat in the full sun for about 8 to 16 hours, depending on the intensity of the sun in your location. Be prepared to defend your meat from scavengers during the process.

Smoking. Cut the meat into thin strips and lay across a rack suspended above a smoky fire. Punk wood (rotten wood that has dried out) is good for making a smoky fire. To speed up the process, gather sticks and build a tepee around the fire, covering the outside of the tepee with some kind of blanketing material. This will direct more heat and smoke toward the meat.

No matter how you decide to store your meat, don't keep meat close to camp. This will attract predators. Tie your meat into a bundle and suspend it from a tall branch away from camp or create a meat safe (from rocks or frozen ground) that keeps animals out of your food stash.

WARNING

Hunting is a risk versus reward activity that you will need to assess in your own survival situation. This activity may open you up to the possibility of an increased number of animal confrontations, but it's important to remember that few animals will attack a human, except in self-defense.

If you're confronted by a wild animal, here are some tips:

- **Avoid eye contact**
- **Freeze (if the animal isn't charging you, *don't run*)**
- **Slowly back off**
- **Avoid sudden movements**
- **If an animal charges, dodge out of the way (you could be blocking their escape route)**

And if the animal attacks:

- **Shout, make a loud noise, and try to make yourself look bigger**
- **Drop whatever you're carrying (it may distract the animal)**
- **If you decide to run, zig-zag as you run away**
- **If a tall tree is close by, climb it**

E: ACTIVITIES TO PRACTICE FOR OBTAINING WILD FOODS

TRACK THE TRACKS

EQUIPMENT REQUIRED:

- **Blank paper**
- **Pencils**

Aim: Identify the wildlife that lives in your natural areas from their tracks.

Take some paper and pencils out into nature areas and look for animal tracks. Sand and mud are great places to look for clear prints. Draw what the prints look like onto the paper, and try to guess what made them. Look at the size, shape, and characteristics of the prints. Was it a bird, reptile, mammal? How many prints are on the ground; could it have been more than one animal? What does it look like they were doing there? Take a look around and see if you can spot any animals in the area. Did any of them make the print? If you can't figure out the animal that made the print, do some research on the internet when you get home and see if you can figure it out.

WALKING THE WALK

Aim: Learn how to move quietly through the outdoors.

This skill is beneficial if you decide the hunt your own food and also allows you to learn how to get closer to animals for observation and photos.

Have a look at the ground you'll be walking on. Think about which surfaces are noisy and which ones will be quiet to walk on. Look at the difference between green leaves and grasses and dead leaves and grasses. Look at how you should place your feet on the ground to make the least amount of noise. Good stalkers place their feet toe-first and then let the rest of their foot touch the ground. Try to walk from a Point A to Point B without making a sound.

See how close you can get to a flock of birds or your pet dog without the animals noticing. Try to get closer each time.

Note: Don't try this with known predators, such as bears or wolves. You may end up becoming the prey.

FISHING

EQUIPMENT REQUIRED:

- **1 fishing rod, or handline and hooks**
- **Bait**
- **1 sharp knife**
- **Cooler or bucket to store the caught fish**

Aim: Learn how to catch and process a fish.

If you live near a body of water, fishing is a great way to learn to catch and process your own food. Ask questions of the local fishing people to find out when they recommend you go fishing and what line and bait to use for the fish in the area. Fishing

shops are also a wealth of knowledge, and the people behind the counter are usually happy to give advice on what gear to use to get the best results. If you're choosing to fish in the ocean, it's better to go fishing when the tide is coming in rather than when the tide is going out, so check your local tide charts to help you decide when to go.

Learn how to set up your own rod and tie on your own hooks. Use the fisherman's knot to attach your hook.

When baiting your hook, again, be careful not to get your fingers caught on the sharp hook, and loop the bait through the hook a few times to make sure it is secure on the hook. If you do get a hook in your skin, seek medical attention—do not try to remove it yourself.

When casting your line, make sure you have stable footing and you aren't on a slippery or steep slope. Check behind you and around you to make sure that no one will be caught in your cast.

Learn the local fish in your area. And be careful removing the fish from your hook, as some species of fish have sharp and poisonous spines; these need to be safely handled to avoid getting cut.

Fish are also good for learning how to gut and clean an animal as they are very simple and usually involve just some de-scaling and a cut down the middle of the stomach to get rid of the guts.

For an added bonus: Cook a fish meal when you get home with your catch.

INVENTING A TRAP

EQUIPMENT REQUIRED:

- **Pencil and paper**
- **An outdoor area with plenty of resources**

Aim: Practice all the elements of a successful trap.

Use the pencil and paper to design a trap and then build that trap in the outdoor area. It may take some experimenting until you have a trigger system and design that would work effectively.

Keep in mind the animals that you have in your local area and what might work best to catch them.

**IMPORTANT: Make sure you trigger your trap once you have finished.*

MAKING A SPEAR

EQUIPMENT REQUIRED:

- **A long, straight stick**
- **A sharp knife**

Aim: Make a spear that could be used for hunting.

A spear is the easiest and best option for weapon-making. You can decide which type of spear you want to make. A simple throwing spear is easiest, and a fishing spear or a knapped-point spear is more complicated.

For a **basic spear**, simply sharpen the end of a long, straight stick into a point. This kind of spear is usually good for thrusting at close range, either for protection or to finish off a kill.

For a **throwing spear**, choose a long, strong, lightweight length of wood. Sharpen the end to a point. You can fire-harden the point by sticking the point under the coals of your fire or rotating it above the flames. I find burying the point under the coals to be more effective, as it hardens the wood without burning it. You can set up a target with a safe, controlled backdrop and throw your spear sticks at the target to see if you can score "dinner."

For a **knapped-point spear**, you can practice making a flake from the Knife section of this book (page 35) and make a split in the narrow end of your long stick. Slide the flake into the split. Make some pitch glue (page 36) and secure the head to the spear using pitch glue and some paracord.

For a **fishing spear**, split the end of the stick into four segments. Sharpen each of these segments individually. Tie two opposing short sticks in the middle of these four segments to create some space between them.

A spear is a weapon, so please use it responsibly. Never throw it toward another person, even if you think you might miss them, and always make sure you can see past your target to make sure your backdrop is clear before throwing.

FORAGING FOR FOOD

EQUIPMENT REQUIRED:

- **A camera, or a sketchbook and pencil**
- **Access to a plant book, plant identifying app, or the internet**

Aim: Learn to identify edible plants in your area.

This is an activity that can be done in your backyard or in any nature area. Challenge yourself to find and identify ten different species of plants. You can identify plants by leaf pattern and type, their height, their flowers, even their nuts or seeds and bark. You can either take photos of these things or sketch them, and use a computer, plant app, or plant book to help identify them. Once the plant has been positively identified, do some research to see if there are any useful properties of the plant. Is it medicinal, nutritious, or helpful in any way? Or is it poisonous and needs to be avoided?

If you live in an area where there are edible plants you can identify, gather them and make something delicious with them. Make sure you have double-checked with a responsible adult prior to consuming, as some edible plants can easily be mistaken for poisonous ones.

F: SURVIVAL MYTHS ABOUT FOOD

1. **If we see an animal eating some kind of vegetation, then it's safe for us to eat.** Most animals have different digestive tracts to our own. This means that some have evolved to process food that may be toxic to humans. For example, the koala lives off eucalyptus leaves, but they are toxic for humans to consume. The only example where it is good to try eating what an animal eats is if you are in a jungle and can find what monkeys are eating. Their digestive tract is most similar to humans and most of what they eat will be edible for you. It is advisable to still perform a Toxin Test prior to consuming, but it will be your safest bet on what to eat.

2. **All wild berries are edible.** While many wild berries are safe to eat, not all of them are. Some wild berries are poisonous and can cause serious illness or death. Only consume berries you can positively identify as safe. For all others, use the Toxin Test to decide if you should consume them or not.

3. **Don't eat slugs or snails.** These little critters can be a great source of food, as they don't run away quickly. With land snails and slugs, it's best to purge them in case they have been eating any vegetation that is toxic to you, so put them in a container with some fresh grass for a few days if possible. Wash thoroughly and boil; cook them in their shells on the open fire or roast them on skewers. Do not eat any snails or slugs that are brightly colored.

10

RESCUE

A: LESSONS FROM THE PAST

In 1994, Mauro Prosperi, an Italian ultra-marathon runner, became lost in the Sahara Desert during the Marathon des Sables race in southern Morocco. Prosperi became disoriented during a sandstorm and ended up running in the wrong direction for several days, becoming severely dehydrated and lost.

After nine days of wandering, the runner came across a Muslim shrine, where he found water and shelter. However, he was still lost and in need of rescue. He used a mirror from his survival kit to reflect sunlight toward a passing military plane, hoping to catch the attention of the pilots. Fortunately, his signal was seen, and he was eventually rescued by a search and rescue team.

If Prosperi hadn't signaled for help using his mirror, he may not have been found in time and could've died in the harsh conditions of the Sahara.

B: THE BEST WAYS TO GET RESCUED

Although the four basic needs of survival are commonly thought of as shelter, water, fire, and food, I include *rescue* under my basic needs because the sooner your survival situation ends successfully, the better for you. This will happen when you figure out how to get out of the situation or when someone finds you.

In a survival situation, it is recommended you remain where you are when your disaster strikes. If remaining there is a threat to your life, then move to somewhere your life isn't in immediate danger. For example, you might need to move because of a capsized boat, a bushfire, or a lack of water.

If your life isn't in immediate danger, staying where you are will give you the best chance to survive. You will not only be closer to where rescuers might start to look for you, but also you won't be potentially moving away from rescuers as they search for you.

I have put myself in challenges where I'm moving and trying to survive, and where I'm staying in the one area and trying to survive—and it is always easier to stay put. When you're on the move, you're burning a lot of calories on an activity other than your immediate survival, and you're losing time that could be used to ensure that you have adequate shelter, water, and food for the night.

Once you've decided you need rescuing and you've taken steps to ensure that shelter, water, and warmth are taken care of, it's time to think about making yourself as visible as possible. How you do this will depend on what resources you have around you and on you. You will need to get inventive. The more visible you can make yourself, the more likely you are to be rescued. Try everything. As silly as it seems, people really have been rescued by putting messages in bottles and floating them out to sea.

SIGNALING

Your rescue is likely to come by means of air, land vehicle, or a rescue mission on foot. You will need to prepare something visible for all of these scenarios. Even if you think you'll hear someone who passes by you on foot, you may be sleeping or out collecting water, and they need to know you're around. Generally, you'll have about two minutes from the time you hear an aircraft to the time it's out of range, so any signaling needs to be thought out beforehand and ready to go.

These things can make you more visible to rescuers:

- **Bright colors**
- **Reflective surfaces**
- **Straight lines and arrows**
- **Words on the ground**
- **Thick smoke**
- **Bright flames**
- **Lights in the dark**

Bright colors. Assuming you have spare gear or clothing with you, hang it from the branches of a high tree, ensuring the leaves don't block the item from view. You could also place the clothing and gear in the middle of a clearing, anchored so it doesn't blow away. Use branches or rocks to make an arrow to indicate the location of your shelter. Use bright green vegetation on darker surfaces to write a message for aerial search parties. Building a tepee structure to hang your bright and colorful pieces from is also a good idea, as the tepee structure itself will attract attention.

Reflective surfaces. While a signal mirror is ideal, assuming you don't have one on you, any reflective surface will do. Use garbage that might be around you, such as polished cans or glass bottles. These will catch the sun's rays, causing a flash of bright light observable from up to two miles away. Hang these pieces in trees around your location. When the wind blows, they will move and signal without you needing to tend them. Also, keep a polished surface on you at all times, in case you hear a vehicle. The front of

a cell phone will work as a reflective surface, even if you are out of signal or your battery has died. Practice reflecting the sun rays until you know how to aim them.

> ***Aerial rescue***—Hold your hand to the sky where the plane is, and direct the light from the sun to your hand. Remove your hand, and you know that the light should be visible from the plane.
>
> ***Ground rescue***—Reflect the light to the ground, and then direct it in a straight line to the vehicle or person.

Keep signaling until you know you've been seen. You'll know you've been spotted when you receive some kind of acknowledgement from the rescue party. It may be in the form of a signal back to you, a change of course, or a low flyover of the aircraft.

Straight lines and arrows. Nature rarely constructs in straight lines, so any structure with straight lines stands out. You can attract attention using lines and arrows made of rocks, branches, or leaves pointing to your location or the direction you are traveling.

Words on the ground. "SOS" was accepted as the worldwide signal for distress in 1906. Although many people believe it is an acronym for something, it was chosen because it translates easily in Morse code (three dots, three dashes, three dots). "HELP" would also work but would require knowledge of the English language. If you are writing words on the ground, make sure you write them in a cleared area, easily visible from above. Make them as large as you can, and try to distinguish them in some way from the ground you are creating them on. Straight-line letters work best, as they don't blend in with nature as easily. Make sure you destroy your words when you're rescued to ensure people don't think someone still needs saving.

Thick smoke. During the day, thick white or black smoke will get attention. If you've managed to get a fire started for your camp, make sure you keep it burning all day, every day. Have separate fires set up for signal fires with dry, extremely flammable fuel ready to go. These fires should be out in the open and large. Fires under trees will be hard to see and may start a forest fire if they get out of control. It's best if you can prepare more than one fire area with three burning fires, which is a universally accepted number for a distress signal. Green leaves will burn with a thick white smoke and anything rubber will burn with a thick black smoke.

Bright flames. For signal fires at night, it's best to have a fire that burns brightly rather than produces smoke. Dry wood and dead leaves will flare up brightly in the dark to shine a light on your location.

Lights in the dark. If have a flashlight with you, save the battery for when you truly need it. Signaling for help is going to be way more useful than having the flashlight on for comfort during the night. Remember your phone screen lights up, and most phones today have a flashlight function, so save your battery if you don't have service. Amplify these lights at night by shining them off something reflective, such as tin cans or shiny surfaces. Three short flashes followed by three long flashes and three short flashes will indicate your distress to anyone in the area. Pause for a minute and signal again.

We have all seen the movies where the hero runs to signal the rescue ship or plane as it moves past their location, only to be too late and watching the rescue pass them by. As focused as you need to be on your basic needs, your overall aim is to get out of your survival situation. So spend the time in the early days of your scenario getting prepared to make the most of any sign of possible help.

C: NAVIGATION

Practicing some basic map reading should be an everyday part of your interaction with the outdoors—even if it is as simple as taking a look at the posted map at a trailhead or checking out

on Google Maps where you are planning to go biking that day. I usually take a photo of the map if I am not planning on carrying a hard copy. Knowing how to find North or the best direction to head toward civilization can help you rescue yourself if the position you find yourself in is less than ideal or if you think that rescue is not going to find you. This may occur when you have gone somewhere that you hadn't told anyone about or changed your plans without telling someone.

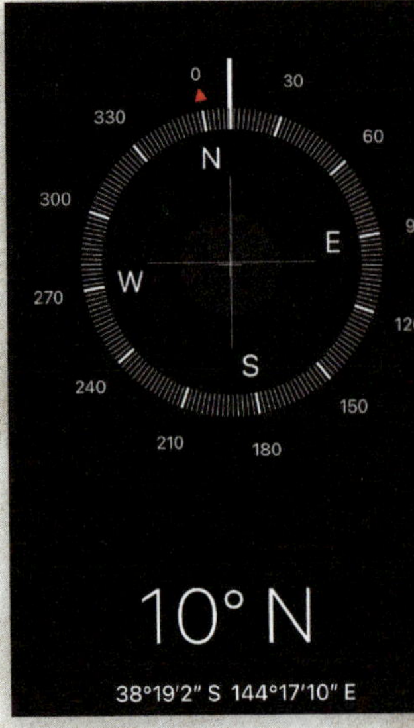

If you've decided that a rescue isn't coming or staying in the area is risking your life, you'll need to leave your initial location. Make a plan about the direction you want to head in based on your best chance of being rescued or making it to civilization. If you had familiarized yourself with your area prior to your emergency, you may have an exact or rough idea of which direction to travel. If you're unsure, heading to a high-point to check out the surrounding terrain is a good idea. Try to locate signs of civilization such as fences, windmills, and rail tracks. Follow your best hope for survival if you're unsure of where to start. In a desert, this will mean following water signs, and in a swamp this may mean heading inland or toward signs of dry land.

If you are on foot, you'll need a system to ensure you walk in a straight line. Humans have a natural tendency to veer to the left or right if they don't have a point to walk toward. This means you'll end up wasting a lot of energy walking in circles. If you don't have a compass and are trying to walk in a set direction, there are a few ways to achieve this. The first is to sight something in the distance that's in the direction you want to go and walk toward that. Once you get to that object, place it at your back and find another object to aim for. This will work in relatively clear terrain but isn't so effective in heavily wooded areas. Another method is using catchment features and "aiming off." This means that you sight a feature you're heading toward that has an obvious feature that funnels to it. This may be a valley pass with a river in front or a farmer's water tank along a fence line. Purposely head to one side of the landmark so that when you're "caught" by the feature, you know to head in a certain direction to get to the landmark.

If you know which direction you want to head in but are unsure how to find that direction or how to stay walking in that direction, some basic map reading skills can help you.

BASIC MAP READING

Usually, maps are aligned toward north. This means the top of the map is north, the bottom is south, the left side is west and the right side, east. The best thing to do first is to line up the map with your world. This can involve laying the map on the ground with the top of the map facing north, or looking at the map photo on your phone with the top of the map photo facing north.

But how to *find* north?

If you have a compass, it's easy. The red needle on the compass always points north (except if you're resting the compass on some kind of metal object like the hood of your car or the metal frame of your back-pack). Smartphones usually have a compass app, which can also show you which way north is. Once you've found north, you may be able to figure out a general direction to travel toward help.

If you don't have a smartphone or compass, the sun will be your next best bet to figure out how to orient your map. The sun rises in the east and sets in the west. At certain times of the year and in different hemispheres, the sun may be in a more northly or southerly direction but will always rise in an easterly direction and set in a westerly direction. Midday is not a good time to try to figure out which way north is, but if it is closer to dawn or dusk, you'll have a better idea. This will give you a rough idea of where north is. For a more accurate north, you can create a sun dial.

SUN DIAL

A sundial can be a useful tool to figure out which way is north. Here's how to create a simple sundial:

1. **Find a flat surface.** You're looking for a flat surface that receives direct sunlight for most of the day. It's best if there's soft ground or an area where you can create a base for a stick to stand in.

2. **Find a straight stick about a foot long.** This will be the part of the sundial that casts a shadow.

3. **Determine the west-east line.** Place the stick vertically in the center of the flat surface, making sure it is straight up and down. Mark the tip of the stick's shadow with a small rock. This marks the west-east line.

4. **Mark the north-south line.** Wait 30 minutes until the shadow moves a little. Mark the tip of the shadow with another small rock. This rock marks the north-south line. Mark a line between the two rocks, and lay a stick to perpendicularly bisect it. This will be your compass.

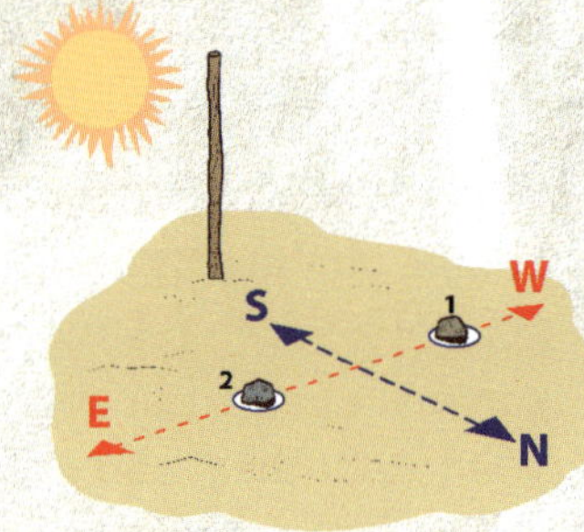

5. **Find north.** Now that you have the west-east and north-south lines marked, you can use them to determine the directions. Stand with your back to the upright stick and your feet on either side of the stick on the ground, and you will be facing a northerly direction.

Once you have found north and oriented your map, you may be able to notice features around you that match those on the map. These features may help guide you toward help.

READING A MAP

Most maps, even the most basic posted maps at trailheads, usually have a key or legend. This is a list of features on the map and the symbols or colors used to portray them. These features may be human-made or natural features and can help you figure where you are on the map. If you can identify where you are and orient the map, you are likely to see which direction you need to travel. If there's a fence line with a gate in only one place on the map and you're at that gate, you should be able to see the best direction to travel.

If you want to find your location on a map using a compass, you will need to get a little more technical. This is where we need to start breaking down the parts of a compass to avoid confusion:

A. **Magnetic north needle**
B. **Bezel**
C. **Baseplate**
D. **Orienting north arrow**
E. **Orienting arrow lines**

FINDING YOUR POSITION WITH A COMPASS

To find your position with a compass, you'll need to follow these steps:

1. Identify a landmark. Look around and identify a prominent landmark, such as a mountain peak, a lake, or a distinctive building.

2. Point the arrow drawn on the front of the compass (not the north arrow) toward the landmark, and spin the bezel until the red lines on the bezel house the red floating north arrow.

3. Place the compass on the map, and line up the map's up-and-down lines with the compass orienting lines and the edge of the compass lined up with the landmark you have identified.

4. Draw a line along the edge of the compass with a pencil.

5. Find another landmark and repeat the process. Where the two lines intersect should be where you are, both on the map and in real life.

FINDING WHERE YOU WANT TO GO WITH A COMPASS

This is called "taking a bearing."

1. **Find your starting point. Identify your location on the map, and place your compass on the map with the edge of the baseplate lined up with your location.**

2. **Set your bearing. Rotate the bezel until the orientating lines run north/south with the ones on the map.**

3. **Take your compass off the map, and line the magnetic north up with the bezel north. Walk in the direction that the baseboard-orientating arrow points.**

This information barely touches on the essentials of map reading and using a compass, so I highly encourage you to learn more and practice whenever you can.

Remember: If you have found yourself in a survival scenario, the best thing to do is stay where you are. Only leave that area if it is dangerous or life-threatening to stay. And make sure you make a plan and use whatever navigation you can to guide you toward your best chance of rescue.

D: ACTIVITIES TO PRACTICE FOR RESCUE

MIRROR, MIRROR

EQUIPMENT REQUIRED:

- **A small mirror**

Aim: Practice aiming the sun's rays toward a target.

Mirrors can be used to reflect sunlight to attract attention from rescuers. Use your mirror to reflect the sun at certain targets, such as a tree truck or a rock on the ground. This will get you used to aiming the mirror toward potential rescuers. It's important to remember you shouldn't direct the light into another person's eyes, as this may cause permanent damage.

SIGNAL FIRE

EQUIPMENT REQUIRED:

- **A small fire**
- **Green leaves**
- **Other flammable organic materials**

Aim: Quickly create a smoky fire.

Start from scratch with your fire-making, and construct a fire that can get started quickly and consistently with methods mentioned in the Fire chapter of this book.

Experiment with different organic material to see which items create the smokiest fire. Green leaves are usually the best method to create smoke quickly, but punky wood (rotten, dry, sponge-like wood) can also be quite good for smoke.

A SIGNAL STRUCTURE

EQUIPMENT REQUIRED:

- **3 long, straight sticks**
- **Shiny objects found in the local area**
- **Paracord or string**

Aim: Create a signal tower using objects found around you.

Take a walk around your local park or outdoor area, and collect objects that may be bright enough to catch the sunlight or attract attention. Place the three sticks into a teepee shape, and tie the top of the sticks together to create a sturdy structure. Tie the shiny and bright objects to the teepee to create an eye-catching backyard sculpture.

MAKE A SUNDIAL

EQUIPMENT REQUIRED:

- **1 straight stick, about a foot long**
- **2 "markers" (small rocks would work)**

Aim: Create a natural way of finding North

A sundial can be a useful tool for figuring out which way is north. Here's how to create a simple sundial:

1. **Find a flat surface.** You're looking for a flat surface that receives direct sunlight for most of the day. It's best if there's soft ground or an area where you can create a base for a stick to stand in.

2. **Find a straight stick about a foot long.** This will be the part of the sundial that casts a shadow.

3. **Determine the west-east line.** Place the stick vertically in the center of the flat surface, making sure it is straight up and down. Mark the tip of the stick's shadow with a small rock. This marks the west-east line.

4. **Mark the north-south line.** Wait 30 minutes until the shadow moves a little. Mark the tip of the shadow with another small rock. This rock marks the north-south line. Mark a line between the two rocks, and lay a stick to perpendicularly bisect it. This will be your compass.

5. **Find north.** Now that you have the west-east and north-south lines marked, you can use them to determine the directions. Stand with your back to the upright stick and your feet on either side of the stick on the ground, and you will be facing a northerly direction. Once you have found north and oriented your map, you may be able to notice features around you that match those on the map. These features may help guide you toward help.

MAPPING THE WAY

EQUIPMENT REQUIRED:

- **A good paper map of an area with a walking trail**
- **A compass**
- **A pencil**
- **Daypack full of all the recommended items for a day hike**

Aim: Always know where you are on a map during your chosen hike.

A good way to practice compass use is to navigate a trail that is already established, taking care to know exactly where you are on the trail at all times. Keep the map and compass out as you walk, and take note of the changes of direction on the path. Try to decide where on the map you are, based on the direction you are now traveling. Mark the spot on the map with a pencil. When you reach a defined feature on the trail, see if you were correct. Don't get discouraged if you make a few mistakes. Navigation is a skill that requires practice.

E: SURVIVAL MYTHS ABOUT RESCUE

1. **A plane in the distance won't be able to see you.** In general, a good signal mirror can be seen from up to 100 miles away, so it's important to start signaling when the plane first comes into sight to try and attract attention. Make sure you mix up the flashes so that the searchers can see you're giving off a purposeful signal and it's not just the light catching off something. Three short flashes followed by three long flashes and three short flashes again will send an internationally recognizable emergency signal in Morse code.

2. **SOS stands for "Save Our Souls."** There have been many meanings associated with the letters SOS over the years. Some people believe it stands for "Save Our Ship" or "Save Our Souls," phrases leftover from the early sailing days. The letters SOS are simply the quickest letters to type out in

Morse code and came about as the distress signal for their convenience. ... --- ...

3. **Following animal tracks is a good way to find your way to help.** Following animal tracks may actually lead you deeper into wilderness areas. Animals wander everywhere in the outdoors. Sometimes animals are heading for food or water, and sometimes they are following ancient migratory routes. Their tracks may lead you to water, but they may also lead you away from where you need to go.

BASIC WILDERNESS FIRST AID

No survival book would be complete without a section on wilderness first aid. But keep in mind that reading about how to do something is no substitute for hands-on experience in a course taught by professionals. This section is here for emergencies or to jog your memory if you have forgotten what to do in the heat of the moment.

A: LESSONS FROM THE PAST

In 2015, Donovan was camping alone and preparing food in the Desolation Wilderness in California when he accidentally cut his arm with his knife. The cut was deep, and he began to lose a lot of blood.

Fortunately, Donovan had received first aid training and knew how to control the bleeding. He used his T-shirt to apply pressure to the wound to stop the bleeding. He then hiked back to his car, despite feeling weak and dizzy from the blood loss.

Once he reached his car, Donovan drove himself to the hospital, where he received treatment for his injury. If he hadn't known how to control the bleeding, he likely would have died from blood loss.

B: DRSABC

This handy acronym will help you remember your order of priorities in a first aid scenario.

DANGER

The last thing you want in an emergency scenario is to put a healthy person in danger. Once you also become a victim, chances of survival diminish. As soon as you see a person in trouble or if you come across someone who looks injured, check the area for danger. What caused the injury? Is it something that will cause injury to you? Has the danger passed, or can you safely remove the victim from danger?

If you've seen someone fall to the ground because a branch broke, it should be safe for you to move toward them and help immediately. If someone has fallen because of a rockslide, wait until the slide has settled before you move in to help them.

Always take a moment to assess the scene. You may want to jump in and rescue someone from danger, but acting *proactively* will usually have a better result than acting *impulsively*. You can see this play out with people who drown as they try to rescue loved ones from ocean rip tides. If they'd taken a moment to grab a flotation device before entering the water, their success would almost be guaranteed. Diving in without one ends up putting two lives in danger.

RESPONSE

Once you've established there is no danger to either party, it's time to assess the patient's level of consciousness. If the person is yelling or screaming, their airway is clear, and they have a pulse. Move on to your secondary assessment.

If the person isn't moving or talking, try to get a response from them. Don't shake them violently, because you don't know what else may be wrong with them. Simply touch their shoulder and ask some questions: "Hello, can you hear me? What's your name? Can you squeeze my hand?" Give them a moment to respond. If they moan in agreement, open their eyes, or answer a question, you can move on to your next assessment.

If there is no response, assume they are unconscious and roll them into the recovery position (more on this in a moment). If the person was injured from a long fall or a knock on the head, assume their spine may be damaged. Take extra care as you move them into the recovery position, and keep the spine straight, if possible.

THE RECOVERY POSITION

An unconscious person is placed in this position, as it allows the airways to stay open and fluids to drain out if need be. The tongue muscle may fall back and block the airways of an unconscious person on their back. To move someone into the recovery position, lie them on their back, bend the arm nearest to you so that their hand cushions their head, and bend the opposite knee to you. Pull the person over onto their side so that their knee holds them on their side. Tilt their head back slightly to ensure their airways are open.

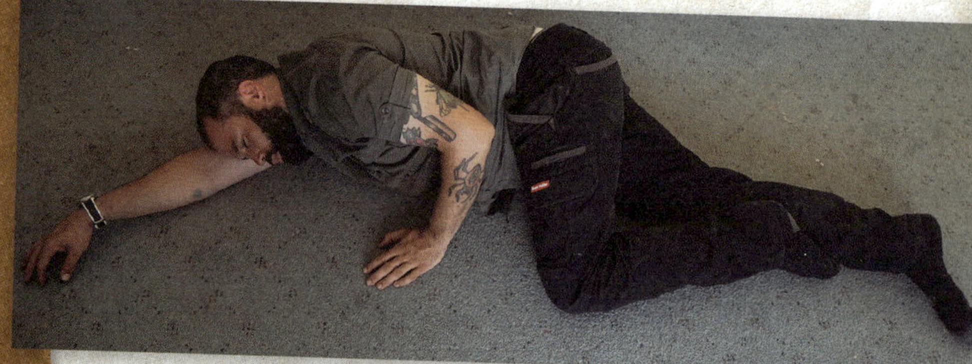

SEND FOR HELP

This is a recent addition to first aid teachings, because it's a step that people in urban environments often forget to do. If you're with a group of people and have access to cell phone service, this is the moment when you delegate someone to call 911. If you're by yourself, take a second to dial, put the phone on speaker, and continue with your assessment.

In a wilderness environment, calling for emergency help can get tricky. If you have cell service, dial 911. If you don't have service where you are and you are dealing with a patient all on your own, continue with your assessment. It is best to get more information and treat the patient to the best of your ability before you head off for help.

AIRWAY

Look to see if you can see any obstructions in the mouth. Scoop out anything that you see inside their mouth that shouldn't be there. If their breathing is wheezy or noisy, there may be something blocking their airway. Do not shove your fingers too far down their throat to try to clear out the obstruction, as this will trigger the gag reflex. If you can't see anything, check their breathing.

BREATHING

If the airway is clear, check for breathing. This can be done by listening, looking, and feeling. Place the back of your hand by their mouth to see if you can feel air moving. Place your hand high on their chest to see if you can feel a rise and fall. Listen to see if you can hear their breath moving in and out.

If the person is breathing, keep them on their side and continue to do your secondary assessment.

If the person isn't breathing, turn them onto their back and commence CPR. This would be the time I would recommend sending someone for help if you are out of cell phone range. If you are alone with the patient, stay with the patient and continue to the next step if neither of these options is available.

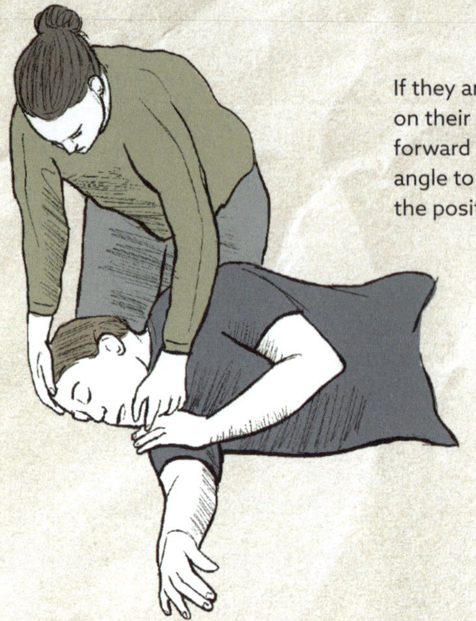

If they are unconscious, place them on their side, with their top leg bent forward and their top arm at a right angle to their body to help maintain the position.

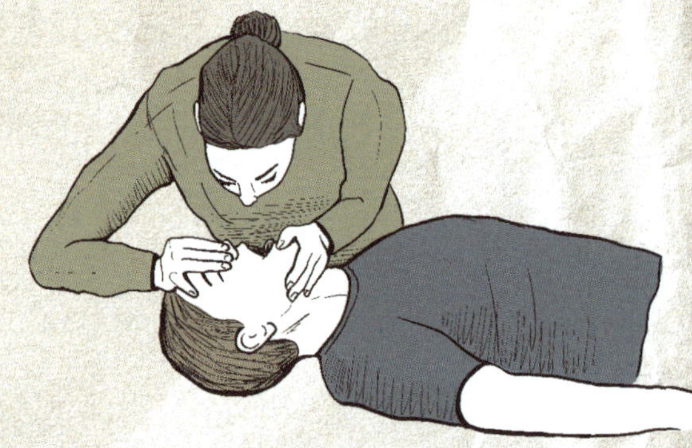

Check to see if their airway is clear.

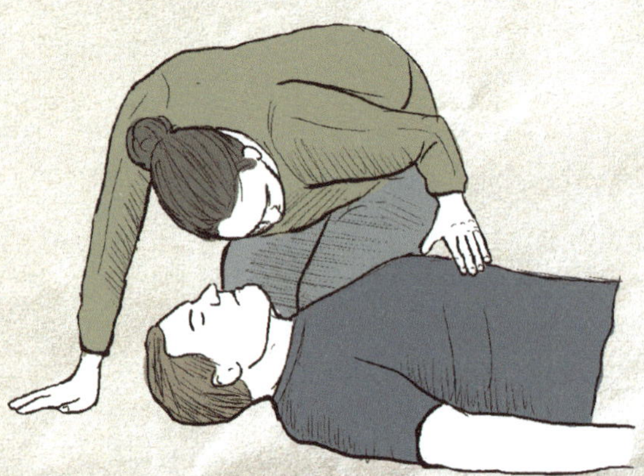

Place your hand on their chest to see if you can feel their chest rise and fall.

COMPRESSIONS

There are many schools of thought as to how many compressions per minute and how many rescue breaths someone should receive during CPR. But as long as you're doing compressions and breaths so the patient's blood is continuing to circulate through the body and oxygen can get to the brain, you are doing more than nothing. 30 compressions to two breaths is considered fairly standard.

How to do chest compressions:

- Kneel by the person's side.
- Place the heel of one hand in the center of the person's chest.
- Place the heel of your other hand on top of the first hand.
- Interlock your fingers.
- Position yourself vertically above the person's chest.
- Keep your arms straight and press down on the sternum until you reach about three inches of depth.
- Keep a pace of approximately 100 compressions per minute.

How to perform assisted breathing:

- Pinch the soft part of the person's nose closed.
- Tilt their head back slightly.
- Use a pinch grip to raise their chin.
- Take a normal breath, and place your lips around the person's lips, creating a seal.
- Blow steadily into their mouth while watching to see if the chest rises.
- Remove your mouth, and let the chest fall.
- Take another normal breath and blow into the person's mouth.

If the chest isn't rising when you breathe into the person's mouth, try tilting the head back a little more or look for an obstruction in their airway. If you don't know the person or feel uncomfortable doing the assisted breathing, it's okay to just do chest compressions.

You will need to continue CPR until the person is breathing on their own, a medical professional has arrived to take over, or your health and safety are compromised. You may be able to swap in and out with other people if you aren't alone, allowing for some rest between rounds.

A person will either recover and start breathing or they won't. In a wilderness setting, if they recover, you'll need to get this person to medical attention as soon as possible. Either get help to come to you, or assess and evacuate on your own. It is important to understand that chances of resuscitation are slim without intervention from either a defibrillator or a professional medical team. Do not feel like you have failed if you are unable to resuscitate someone. The failure would have been in not possessing the knowledge to at least try.

SECONDARY ASSESSMENT

Once you have completed your DRSABC and the person is conscious or unconscious but breathing, you will need to check what else has to be done to keep them alive. This is where the scenarios become too numerous for me to list off. There are situations that need to be dealt with immediately or the person will deteriorate, such as deadly bleeds and venomous snake bites, and situations that are not so urgent like blisters and splinters. Generally, a conscious person will be able to describe what has happened to them, which will cut down the guesswork of what you need to treat. It will also be easier to assess their needs if you were around them when they became unconscious. It is only when you come across an unconscious person that you will need to do some investigation as to the possible cause.

This secondary assessment will include looking, feeling, and asking questions (if the victim is conscious).

C: DEADLY BLEEDS AND WOUNDS

A severed artery can lead to someone bleeding out in minutes. It doesn't take much of a cut to sever an artery. I've lost count of the times I have seen people cutting something with a knife while resting the object on their leg. Fatigue and momentary lapses in concentration can have disastrous consequences when combined with sharp objects or projectiles.

Deadly bleeds are wounds where the blood is pumping from the wound, the bleeding doesn't slow down or stop with pressure, and/or the blood is quickly soaking through the bandage. Deadly bleeds can be internal or external. External ones are more obvious, as there will be blood soaking their clothing or flowing from the wound. Internal bleeds can generally be observed as swelling or bruising at an impact site. If the swelling or bruising is in the abdominal region, call for help and evacuate as soon as possible because bleeding organs can result in a rapid death.

For all deadly bleeds, immediate evacuation and medical assistance will be required. Treat the wound first before dialing emergency services if you're alone or only with the victim. If you're in a group, assign someone else to dial or head out for help immediately.

If the object is still in the body, do not attempt to remove it. If it is protruding from the wound, immobilize it in place so it doesn't move around and create further damage internally. Removing projectiles in the wilderness could open up arteries and the patient can bleed out in minutes.

The first thing to do with a massive bleed is to apply pressure to the wound. Grab some absorbent material if you have any available or use your hands to try to stem the bleeding. In some cases, wounds will stop bleeding when pressure is applied to them. Elevate the wound above the level of the heart if possible. If you have absorbent dressing and a bandage available, place the dressing on the wound and wrap in place with a bandage. You want a firm bandage but not a tourniquet. If the wound bleeds through the dressing, do not remove the initial dressing, simply apply another layer of absorbent material and another bandage.

WOUNDED LIMB

If the wound is deep and to a limb, apply pressure, elevate the area above the heart, and cover with a pressure bandage, making sure that it is firm but not tight enough to cut off pressure to the extremities.

ABDOMINAL WOUND

If the wound is in the abdomen, and there are no internal organs visible, treat as above. If there are internal organs visible or protruding, *do not try to stuff them back into the cavity.* Cover the wound with a moist, sterile dressing and bandage firmly. Make the victim comfortable but do not give them anything to eat or drink.

CHEST WOUND

If the wound is in the chest and a wheezing noise can be heard through the wound, assume a lung has been punctured. Cover the hole with a dressing that can create a pressure seal. This can be a Ziploc bag or something similar. Tape around three edges of the square, allowing one side to remain free. Immobilize the victim until help can arrive.

TOURNIQUET

Unless a limb has been completely shattered or torn off or the femoral artery (the main artery in your leg) has been compromised, try to avoid applying a tourniquet. A tourniquet is a last resort, as it will probably result in the loss of a limb once applied in the field. If your choice is to lose a life or lose a limb, apply a tourniquet and do not take it off. Write the time and date that you applied it. The only person who should remove a tourniquet is a medical professional.

D: BREAKS AND SPRAINS

BROKEN BONE

It may be hard to tell the difference between a sprained joint and a broken bone. Some things to look for that signify a break will be deformities, numbness, and whether the patient heard a cracking noise when the injury occurred. Sprains will usually be associated with a popping noise. Depending which bone is broken, the patient may be able to walk out unaided or will not be able to support their weight at all. If the patient is unable to put weight on the injured limb, take the weight off, apply a compression bandage, and have them rest in the position most comfortable to them. If you have cold water available, soak a bandana in the water and cover the injured area with a cooling compress.

SPRAINS

These usually occur in the ankle and can range from a slight twist, which is easily walked off, to more extreme tendon and ligament damage. Assess the severity of the sprain. If you aren't far from your exit and the person is able to put weight on the ankle, do not remove their footwear. It is acting as a compression bandage and supporting the injury. Provide some aid in the form of a walking stick or a shoulder to lean on, and together slowly make your way to safety. If the victim is unable to put weight on the injured foot, take the weight off, remove their footwear, apply a compression bandage and have them rest with their foot elevated. If you have cold water available, soak a bandana in the water and cover the foot with a cooling compress.

E: BITES AND STINGS

If something bites you and you get ill, it is venomous. If you bite something and you get ill, it is poisonous. This section will look at how to deal with venom.

SNAKES

When a snake strikes, usually the venom will enter the body in the lymphatic system. Lymph is a clear fluid located between your skin and muscles that moves rapidly through the body only when you move your muscles. This means the first action in dealing with a snake bite is to stay calm and still. Get out of the way of the snake and away from danger, and then lay down in a comfortable position. Make sure the heart is higher than the bite site, if possible. Immobilize the limb with the bite. If you are close to help, do not wash the venom off the wound, as medical professionals will use this sample to identify the antivenom they need to treat the victim. Simply cover the wound with non-adhesive dressing and, using a compression bandage, wrap from the joint below the bite to the joint above the bite. The bandage should be firm but not cut off circulation. Mark on the bandage where the bite is. Call or send for help. Do not attempt to move the patient.

ALL OTHER BITES AND STINGS

Monitor the site of the injury for changes. If you've been bitten or stung by a land insect, put a cooling compress on the more serious stings. Having an insect bite relief cream or spray in your first aid kit is a good idea.

If there are any signs or symptoms of an allergic reaction, such as swelling of the throat or wheezing, rashes, hives, or severe swelling at the bite site, take an antihistamine and look to head home. If you are traveling with anyone who has a known extreme allergic reaction, make sure that they bring their EpiPen and keep it at the top of their pack.

To treat a sting from a marine animal, you need warm water—as hot as the patient can bear. Marine animals have some of the most toxic venom in the world, so if you've been stung in a marine environment, evacuate and seek professional medical help as soon as possible.

F: HEAT AND COLD INJURIES

BURNS

Sitting around an open campfire at night is associated with most camping and wilderness experiences. It's easy to forget that a pot might still be hot if you pick it up, or that burning log can roll out of the fire and make contact with skin. Depending on the severity of the burn, you may need to evacuate to get medical help immediately, or simply run the burn under cold water for ten minutes to ease the pain so you can continue your trip.

The important thing to remember with burns is that the layers of skin continue to burn after the heat source is removed. Because of this, skin that is burned requires immediate cooling, preferably under running cold water for at least ten minutes. Keep cooling the area until removing from the water doesn't lead to an increase in pain or until water isn't providing any further relief.

Burns extending over 50 percent or more of the body are usually fatal. In case of these burns, call or send for emergency help, and try to submerge the victim in cool running water for at least ten minutes.

DIFFERENT TYPES OF BURNS:

- ***First-degree.*** These are mild compared to other burns; they cause pain and reddening of the outer layer of skin.
- ***Second-degree.*** These are partial-thickness burns that affect the outer layer and the lower layer of skin; they cause pain, redness, swelling, and blistering.
- ***Third-degree.*** These are full-thickness burns that go through the skin layers and affect deeper tissues; they result in white or black charred skin that may be numb.
- ***Fourth-degree.*** These go deeper than third-degree burns and can affect your muscles and bones; nerve endings are also damaged or destroyed, so there is no feeling in the burned area.

Third- and fourth-degree burns require immediate evacuation. Cool with running water for ten minutes, and cover area with a dry nonstick adhesive dressing. Do not apply anything else to the burn. Hydrate the victim by ensuring they continue to sip small amounts of water.

Second-degree burns will require assessment. Any burn that is larger than an inch in diameter should be cooled in running water and covered with dry, sterile dressing; the victim should then be evacuated to medical help. If you have a burn-specific dressing or gel, it is okay to apply this if you don't have cold running water, or when you are evacuating. Do not burst blisters. They are keeping the burn site sterile and reducing the chance of infection.

First-degree burns can be cooled under cold running water and monitored. Do not apply any oil-based products, as these can heat up and "cook" the area further.

ENVIRONMENT-RELATED INJURY

These are any injuries to the body caused by the climate or ecosystem you are in.

Dehydration – when the body has lost too much water and other fluids that it needs to work properly. Signs and symptoms include:

- **Dry mouth**
- **Tiredness or fatigue**
- **Thirst**
- **Lack of urination (you should be peeing once every few hours)**
- **Dark-colored pee**
- **Headache**
- **Dizziness**

If untreated, dehydration can progress into foggy thinking, an inability to make rational decisions. Eventually symptoms can progress to seizures, brain damage, and even death. Stop, rest in the shade, and hydrate until symptoms begin to ease.

Heat exhaustion. This condition is the result of your body overheating. Signs and symptoms of heat exhaustion include:

- **Cool, moist skin with goose bumps (when you're in the heat)**
- **Heavy sweating**
- **Faintness**
- **Dizziness**
- **Fatigue**
- **Weak, rapid pulse**
- **Low blood pressure**
- **Muscle cramps**

The best cure for heat exhaustion is to cool the body down. So stop any activity, seek shelter, and drink water if you have it. Preventing heat exhaustion is better than having to cure it, so try not to be active in the heat of the day.

Heat stroke. If heat exhaustion is untreated, it will lead to heat stroke. This is the most serious heat-related illness and occurs when the body becomes unable to control its temperature. Body temperature may rise to 106°F or higher in 10 to 15 minutes. Signs and symptoms of heat stroke include:

- **Throbbing headache**
- **Lack of sweating, despite the heat**
- **Red skin that's hot and dry**
- **Nausea and vomiting**
- **Rapid heartbeat**
- **Rapid, shallow breathing**
- **Confusion and disorientation**
- **Seizures**
- **Unconsciousness**

Cool the body down as soon as possible. Stop any activity, seek shade, and use water to wet skin while actively fanning to reduce core temperature.

Hypothermia. This condition occurs when the body loses heat faster than it can produce heat. It's better to prevent hypothermia than try to cure it in the field, so always begin to try to warm yourself when you start to feel cold.

Signs and symptoms of hypothermia include:

- **Shivering**
- **Slurred speech or mumbling**
- **Slow, shallow breathing**
- **Weak pulse**
- **Clumsiness or lack of coordination**
- **Drowsiness**
- **Confusion**
- **Loss of consciousness**

Someone with hypothermia usually isn't aware of their condition, as the symptoms come on gradually. Eventually hypothermia can lead to risk-taking behavior and a feeling of euphoria. Quite often people who have died of cold exposure are found naked, as they begin to feel overheated and take all their clothes off in the final stages of the condition.

When you start to feel cold, add layers or remove damp clothing and replace with dry. Move around, seek shelter and warmth. Do not attempt to warm hypothermia patients quickly, as this will lead to cold blood in the extremities rushing to the core and dropping the core temperature dangerously. Warm drinks and a hot water bottle on top of a layer of clothing by their core will help. It is not recommended that another person strip their clothes and join the patient because this may lead to two cold people instead of two warm people. But if you're having trouble warming the patient, keep on your warm layer and get close to them.

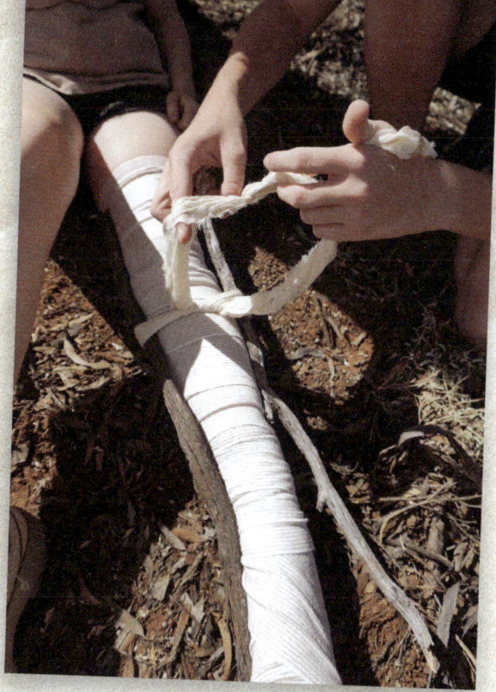

G: SPLINTS

If you have assessed the injury and decided that the best treatment for the comfort of the patient would be to immobilize the limb, it requires a splint. You will need to:

- **Find suitable materials.** Look around for materials that can be used to make a splint. These can include sticks, branches, trekking poles, or any other sturdy items you can find.
- **Pad the splint.** Once you've found suitable materials, pad the splint with soft materials like clothing, moss, or leaves to provide cushioning for the injured area.
- **Secure the splint.** Use a strong material like duct tape or rope to secure the splint. Make sure it's tight enough to hold the splint in place, but not so tight that it restricts circulation.
- **Check circulation.** After the splint is in place, check the circulation in the injured area. Make sure there is no numbness, tingling, or discoloration of the skin, which could indicate a problem with circulation.

H: EVACUATION

If you've assessed that the ill or injured person is stable but requires further medical help, you may need to self-evacuate. This should only be done if you're unable to get medical help to you, and/or if moving the individual will not compromise their life or their injury. It can also be done if not moving them will compromise their life.

You will have to take into consideration:

- **The type of injury sustained**
- **The distance you need to travel to get to help**
- **The type of terrain you need to move through**
- **The people available to help you**
- **The individual's weight**
- **The resources available to make a carrying device**
- **The fitness of the people evacuating**

Always test your evacuation system with a healthy person, if possible, before moving the person who needs to be evacuated.

There are many different methods of creating a support for a someone incapable of walking out of the wilderness on their own. You may need to get creative. And keep in mind that the support needs to be strong and as comfortable as you can make it to prevent secondary injuries.

SOLO EVACUATION

If there are only two people—one healthy person and one who is not—you will need to assess the weight and build of the injured person compared to the weight and build of the healthy person. Injuring a healthy person or dropping an injured person makes the first aid scenario worse. I don't recommend carrying someone in your arms or across your shoulders unless you don't have far to go, the terrain is flat, or the person is a young child or toddler.

BACKPACK CARRY

If you have a backpack with you, even a large daypack, you have a frame capable of supporting heavy weight in a position that will create the least impact on the person carrying. Loosen the arm straps of the pack all the way, and have the patient step through the arm loops with the bag at their back. Lean forward and have that person get on your back, threading your arms through the arm loops. Tighten the waist strap around your waist, and cinch in the arm straps so they are between you and the backpack, and their weight is mostly on your waist strap. Walk out.

SLING CARRY

You will need something long enough to go around both you and the patient and wide enough that it doesn't cut into your skin. A tarp or sleeping sheet works. Roll into a line and tie the ends together, forming a loop. Have one side of the loop sitting under the person's buttocks and one across their back. Loop your arms through so that the person being carried is in a supported piggyback position on your back.

EVACUATION WITH MORE THAN TWO PEOPLE

Having just one other person to help with the evacuation eases the load immensely. The two-person carrying methods I recommend for a conscious patient are the arm seat or the backpack assist. Only use the arm seat method if you don't have far to travel. If the person is unconscious or unable to support themselves, you will have to build a stretcher. If you have a larger group, take turns being the carriers and take rest breaks as needed.

ARM SEAT

The two carriers grip hand to wrist, creating a square "seat" for the victim. The victim sits with an arm over each of the carriers' shoulders.

BACKPACK ASSIST

If there are two backpacks available, have the two carriers put on the packs and tuck a solid stick above the waist band of the packs suspended between the two carriers. The victim will sit on the stick and sling an arm over each of the carriers' shoulders.

STRETCHER

The aim with a stretcher is that you make it as light and as strong as you can. If you only have two people to carry it, you don't want to add any more weight to the structure than you have to, as carrying a stretcher is a physically demanding task. You'll need two poles about two feet longer than the patient's body length. The middle support can be any number of things from backpacks to jackets or sweaters with the poles threaded through. If you have rope, you can weave a hammock for the middle; duct tape works great as well. Get creative, but make sure that the stretcher is wide enough to fit the victim's shoulders. Ensure their comfort by lining the stretcher with sleeping bags or extra clothes.

Evacuations pose all kinds of risk for both the injured party and the healthy people assisting. Only perform evacuation if you don't have far to travel or it is your last resort. Otherwise, make the patient as comfortable as possible and wait for rescue.

I: WHAT'S IN YOUR FIRST AID KIT?

A first aid kit should be an essential on every trip into the outdoors. I take a smaller first aid kit on day trips and a more extensive kit if I'm doing a multiday trip or leading expeditions. My kit also changes depending on where I'm traveling and what sort of conditions I may face.

A first aid kit is designed to deliver the first line of aid in a medical emergency. But simply buying a first aid kit is not enough. You need to be thoroughly familiar with what your kit contains and how to use all of the kit's contents.

A first aid kit should be red and clearly marked as a first aid kit. A good kit should include:

- **1 major wound dressing:** this has a thick absorbent pad attached to a bandage, ready to place and apply pressure on a deadly wound
- **1 triangular bandage:** to create a sling, help apply pressure, and to aid in head bandaging; they can also be soaked in cold water and used for a cold compress
- **1 pressure bandage:** in case of snake bites and sprains
- **6 safety pins:** to fasten slings or bandages
- **1 roll hypoallergenic sports tape:** to provide support for injuries
- **6 small conforming bandages:** to keep dressings in place
- **10 nonadherent wound dressings:** for burns and abrasions
- **5 combine dressings:** for major wounds
- **5 cotton gauze swabs:** for wound cleaning
- **20 adhesive dressings:** for minor scrapes, cuts, and blisters
- **Antiseptic wipes:** to clean minor wounds and scrapes
- **1 ice pack:** for applying to sprains or breaks or to help cool down burns and scalds if you don't have access to cold running water
- **2 saline solutions:** for washing wounds or irrigating eyes
- **4 sets of plastic gloves:** to prevent the exchange of bodily fluids and to keep the injury site as clean as possible

- **1 emergency blanket:** for cold exposure
- **1 pair tweezers:** for removing small, embedded objects
- **3 Hydralyte:** to aid in rehydration

Make sure to include any prescription medication that you require.

I can't stress enough the importance of completing a first aid course and carrying a first aid kit into the outdoors with you. Chances are, you won't be the one who benefits from your training—your knowledge could mean the difference between life and death for someone you care about.

J: FIRST AID ACTIVITIES

SNAKE BITE BANDAGE

EQUIPMENT REQUIRED:

- **2 compression bandages**
- **1 marker**

Aim: Learn how to quicky and efficiently apply a compression bandage in case of a snake bite.

Always assume that any snake bite is venomous, unless you are 100 percent certain of your snake ID.

The idea of the compression wrap is to restrict the lymph flow and slow down—but not stop—the blood flow from the area. There's a fine line between a wrap that's "firm" and "too tight," so it is a good idea to practice when there's no pressure to get it right.

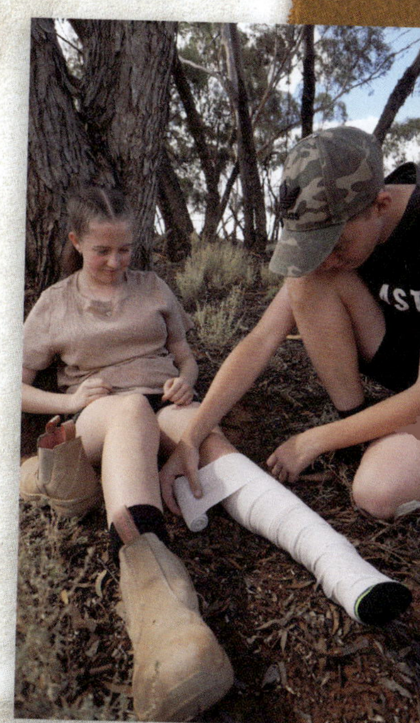

Draw two dots on the patient's skin to symbolize a snake bite. Start wrapping just below the joint farthest away from the torso on the bitten limb. Wrap firmly, but not tightly, from the joint below the bite to the joint above the bite, wrapping toward the torso. Get your patient's feedback on the pressure of the bandage. If they complain of tingling or numbness, the bandage is too tight. If they lose circulation in their fingers, the bandage is too tight. If they can freely move their limb, the bandage is too loose.

IMPROVISE A SPLINT

EQUIPMENT REQUIRED:

- **Whatever you have on you or around you**

Aim: Comfortably splint a limb for an "injured" patient using whatever you can find.

I would try this in an indoor setting where you have access to a lot of equipment, and also in an outdoor setting where you may have a limited selection of human-made items and have to get creative with natural resources.

Choose to splint an arm or a leg. These days the First Aid Rule of Thumb is to splint the limb in the position that's most comfortable to the patient, so remember to ask them how it feels best for their limb to be supported. The splint should protect the limb from further movement but should also be comfortable for the patient. I recommend padding the limb between the splint material and their limb. The splint must be tied firmly to minimize movement. Try to leave a toe or finger accessible during the splinting, so you can check circulation to make sure that the splint isn't cutting off blood supply to the limb.

BUILD A STRETCHER

EQUIPMENT REQUIRED:

- **Paracord or rope**
- **Outside resources**

Aim: Build a stretcher using mainly natural resources found outside.

Design and create a stretcher out of mainly resources you can find around you outside, keeping in mind weight, comfort, and ease of carrying. Depending on how many people you can get to help you, try out the stretcher to see how comfortable it is, how far you can carry someone, and how easy it is to move. It's important to support the person on the stretcher at all times. Always communicate your intentions with the whole group, and pick up and place down the stretcher in a uniform way.

K: SURVIVAL MYTHS ABOUT FIRST AID

1. **You should cut into a snake bite and suck to get the venom out.** This is a common myth but may endanger the person who is doing the sucking if they end up with venom in their system via blood and their mouth. In Australia, where I'm from, the snake venom doesn't even travel through the blood system so this definitely won't be effective in treating the patient. The best treatment is to immobilize the limb and seek help immediately.

2. **Using a tourniquet is always necessary to stop major bleeding.** Tourniquets should only be used as a last resort when all other methods of stopping bleeding have failed or when a limb has been removed. They can cause permanent damage to living tissue and should only be used in life-threatening emergencies.

3. **You should pee on jellyfish stings.** In reality, urinating on a jellyfish sting can actually make it worse, because it could cause more venom to be released into the skin. It really depends on how hydrated you are at the time, which is hard to tell in the heat of the moment. The best method to treat a jellyfish sting is to pour white vinegar on the attached tentacles, remove them with tweezers, and then soak in water as warm as you can bear. Depending on the jellyfish and the amount of associated pain, it may also be best to seek medical advice.

IN SUMMARY

The world of survival and outdoor skills is infinite. I've been studying it my whole life and still learn something new every time I go into the outdoors. This book has only touched the surface of all the amazing things to be discovered out there. It contains subjects that I consider important, but if you get hooked on improving your survival skills, there's much more to be learned.

Remember to always try things for yourself and don't necessarily trust the experts, not even me. Something may work for you that didn't work for me. And above all else, remember that even if your skillset doesn't seem up to the challenge, your mindset may well be. Never give up.

QUIZ: WOULD YOU SURVIVE?

1. **The four attitudes of survival are:**

   a. Be grateful, be aware, be happy, be fun
   b. Be positive, be educated, be prepared, be adaptable
   c. Be positive, be adventurous, be prepared, be excited
   d. Be adaptable, be adventurous, be quiet, be calm

2. **Which one of these is something you can change in a survival scenario?**

   a. The fact you're lost
   b. The fact you're cold
   c. The fact you don't have your phone
   d. The weather

3. **Most people get rescued within:**

   a. One to three days
   b. Three weeks
   c. One week
   d. Three hours

4. **Part of the fight-or-flight response is:**

   a. A boxing move

   b. A quick burst of adrenaline that allows for extra energy in an emergency situation

   c. Something birds do before they eat

   d. A dance move

5. **Some things to include in your daypack for a day hike would be:**

   a. A gallon of water

   b. An emergency blanket

   c. A small first aid kit

   d. All of the above

6. **The Rule of 3s is:**

   a. How many fingers you should hold up to signal you need help

   b. A guide on how to prepare for an outdoor excursion

   c. A rough guide to how long you can last without certain basic needs

   d. A complex algebra equation

7. **You can last roughly three days without:**

   a. Your pet dog

   b. Water

   c. Fire

   d. Food

8. **Which of the following is a survival need?**

   a. Fire

   b. Toilet paper

   c. Cell phone

   d. Map

9. **Your survival priorities are:**

   a. Bathing, sleeping, decorating, talking
   b. Shelter, fire, water, food, rescue
   c. Shelter, sleep, company, fire
   d. Hiking, swimming, food, fire

10. **Your main survival priority is:**

    a. Food
    b. Fire
    c. Dependent on your specific situation
    d. Water

11. **When you first get a knife, it's important that the edge is blunt so you don't cut yourself.**

    a. True b. False

12. **The blood triangle is:**

    a. A werewolf pact
    b. A magic spell
    c. The area you have to be careful to avoid when using a knife
    d. Something you carve into a piece of wood

13. **When choosing a knife:**

    a. Bigger is better
    b. Try to choose one you've seen on TV or social media
    c. The cheapest is best
    d. It should fit comfortably in the palm of your hand

14. **If I don't have my knife in its sheath, then I can put it in the ground to protect the blade.**

    a. True b. False

15. **It's important to put the knife away if:**

  a. You're tired
  b. Someone is within arm's reach of you
  c. You aren't using it
  d. All of the above

16. **When passing a knife to another person, make sure:**

  a. The blade is facing them
  b. They don't see it coming
  c. You hold the knife by the front of the blade, so no one else gets hurt
  d. You hold the knife by the back of the blade and pass it to them handle first

17. **Only a master flintknapper can make a sharp edge out of a rock.**

  a. True b. False

18. **If you don't have a blade, you can make a sharp edge out of:**

  a. Shells
  b. Rocks
  c. Bone
  d. All of the above

19. **How many hours can it take to die in extreme temperatures?**

  a. 1
  b. 2
  c. 3
  d. 4

20. Which one of these is not a way you lose body heat to the environment?

a. Smoldering
b. Convection
c. Evaporation
d. Radiation

21. You are safe to camp in a dry creek bed if:

a. You can't see any rain around
b. It's raining but not where you are
c. It's only sprinkling rain
d. Never

22. Some things to look out for that'll make shelter-building easier are:

a. Fallen trees
b. Caves and overhangs
c. Natural hollows
d. All of the above

23. It's better to build a shelter from scratch so that you know it will be a good one.

a. True   b. False

24. When building a shelter:

a. Make one quickly, even if you will need to make another one later
b. Build it as big as you can
c. Take a moment to assess the best shelter so you only need to build it once
d. Make sure it has lots of holes in the roof so you can look at the stars

25. **What would not be ideal for a shelter?**

    a. A flat area to lie on
    b. Next to running water
    c. Windproof
    d. Waterproof

26. **The first level of shelter is:**

    a. The sky
    b. Your clothing
    c. A cave
    d. A tent

27. **Which of the following would be the best shelter to build in a cold environment?**

    a. Leaf box
    b. Lean-to
    c. Tepee
    d. Reflection wall

28. **You can survive the night in the snow, even if you can't get a fire going.**

    a. True　　**b.** False

29. **Roughly how many days can you survive without water?**

    a. 3
    b. 4
    c. 5
    d. 6

30. Dehydration symptoms can be:

- **a.** Dry mouth
- **b.** Tiredness or fatigue
- **c.** Confusion and dizziness
- **d.** All of the above

31. If you want to prevent water loss:

- **a.** Go for a run
- **b.** Chat with a friend
- **c.** Stay in the shade
- **d.** Eat a big meal of meat

32. When going into the outdoors, it's always better to carry more water than you think you'll need.

a. True **b.** False

33. Which one of these is *not* a way to find water outdoors?

- **a.** Follow animal tracks
- **b.** Dig in a damp area
- **c.** Walk up a dry creek bed
- **d.** Follow smaller, seed eating birds

34. The best water to drink without treating is:

- **a.** Rainwater
- **b.** Saltwater
- **c.** Rapidly flowing creek water
- **d.** Puddles

35. Most water in the outdoors is safe to drink.

a. True **b.** False

36. The most effective way of making water safe to drink in the outdoors is:

a. Straining
b. Shaking
c. Condy's crystals
d. Boiling

37. Charcoal is good for upset stomachs because:

a. It fills you up
b. It absorbs toxins from water
c. It is a painkiller
d. It makes you vomit

38. The best combination of materials for a natural water filter are:

a. Sand, mud, leaves, moss
b. Sand, droppings, mud, charcoal
c. Grass, pebbles, sand, charcoal
d. Grass, wood, leaves, mud

39. In a survival scenario, you should always ration your water to a sip.

a. True **b.** False

40. Which of the following animals is known for putting out campfires?

a. Giraffe
b. Lion
c. Elephant
d. Rhinoceros

41. Which one of the following isn't a good thing to do when practicing making a fire?

- **a.** Clear the area
- **b.** Wait for a windy day
- **c.** Have a water supply handy
- **d.** Tie back long hair

42. Which one of the following isn't a requirement to make fire?

- **a.** Marshmallows
- **b.** Oxygen
- **c.** Fuel
- **d.** Heat source

43. Another name for a tinder bundle is:

- **a.** Stick bag
- **b.** Bird's nest
- **c.** Wood pile
- **d.** Match roll

44. What makes good tinder?

- **a.** Dry cattail heads
- **b.** Dry grass
- **c.** Dried bracket fungus
- **d.** All of the above

45. Which one of the following isn't an important part of fire preparation?

- **a.** Striking a match
- **b.** Making a tinder bundle
- **c.** Preparing the fire site
- **d.** Gathering kindling

46. Which type of wood burns slowly and produces good coals?

a. Soft wood
b. Punky wood
c. Bamboo
d. Hardwood

47. Which one of these is not a method of fire making?

a. Refraction
b. Chemical
c. Rhythmic
d. Percussion

48. Which of these methods of making fire is considered a primitive fire making method?

a. Flint and steel
b. Friction fire
c. Ferro rod
d. Lighter

49. The percussion method of making fire involves:

a. A battery
b. Drumming
c. Two things that, when struck together, create a spark
d. Lightning

50. Wood for a friction fire should ideally be:

a. Green wood
b. Soft, lightweight wood
c. Solid wood with a lot of resin
d. Curved

51. How many people are the minimum required for the strap drill method of fire making?

a. 1
b. 2
c. 3
d. 4

52. The best material for a fire saw is:

a. Balsa wood
b. Pine
c. Bamboo
d. Cattail

53. How long can you last without food?

a. 2 days
b. 3 weeks
c. 3 hours
d. I'm starving by lunchtime

54. All berries are edible.

a. True **b.** False

55. Some plants to avoid if you can't positively identify them are:

a. Mushrooms
b. Beans or bulbs
c. Red plants
d. All of the above

56. Which of the following isn't a step in the Toxin Test?

- **a.** Cook
- **b.** Smell
- **c.** Inspect
- **d.** Check for skin irritation

57. If you've become sick from something you've eaten:

- **a.** Eat some more
- **b.** See if someone else gets sick from it too
- **c.** Drink a lot of water and try to vomit
- **d.** Cook it and try again

58. Which of these is not a common edible plant?

- **a.** Coconuts
- **b.** Bamboo
- **c.** Stinging nettles
- **d.** Oleander

59. There are poisonous seaweeds.

a. True **b.** False

60. One thing that won't change the way an animal track looks is:

- **a.** When it last rained
- **b.** The color of the animal
- **c.** How windy it is
- **d.** How fast the animal is moving

61. Droppings are helpful to look at because they can tell you:

a. What types of animals are in the area
b. What an animal likes to eat
c. When the animal was last there
d. All of the above

62. One thing to think about before hunting an animal is:

a. Nature versus nurture
b. Yin vs yang
c. Risk versus reward
d. Stripes versus spots

63. It's best to avoid eating frogs that are:

a. Brightly colored
b. Loud
c. Very big
d. Very fast

64. Which of these insects are okay to eat?

a. Caterpillars
b. Brightly colored ones
c. Wood grubs
d. Grubs found on the underside of leaves

65. It is okay to eat mollusks if they:

a. Remain partially open when you touch them
b. Are attached to rocks when you find them
c. Smell funny
d. Are cone shaped

66. **Which one of these is not an advantage of passive hunting?**

   a. It takes a lot of time
   b. It allows you to set multiple traps
   c. Traps and snares don't take much energy to set
   d. It works for you when you aren't there

67. **The best trap to set in all survival scenarios is:**

   a. The deadfall trap
   b. The Figure 4 Deadfall
   c. Flexible, depending on your location
   d. The Arapuca Trap

68. **Once you're rescued, you should leave your traps and snares set for the next person who comes along.**

   a. True **b.** False

69. **Which of the following doesn't contribute to a successful deadfall?**

   a. The weight of the deadfall
   b. The color of the deadfall
   c. The density of the ground beneath the deadfall
   d. The speed of the trigger mechanism

70. **Which of the following is the best trap for birds?**

   a. Figure 4
   b. Arapuca
   c. Paiute
   d. Spring snare

71. The best knot for attaching a hook to a line is:

a. Reef knot
b. Fisherman's knot
c. Overhand knot
d. Bow

72. Primitive hooks can be made out of the following:

a. Bone
b. Antler
c. Thorns
d. All of the above

73. When you're active hunting, it is important that you:

a. Stay active
b. Take note of the wind direction
c. Run a lot
d. Make lots of noise so that predators know you're coming

74. If you see an animal eating something, then it's okay for you to eat it too.

a. True   b. False

75. When you're lost, you have the best chance of being rescued if you:

a. Stay where you are
b. Panic
c. Keep moving because you might get somewhere better
d. Build a really big shelter

76. It's important to try to make yourself visible in a survival scenario because:

- **a.** Bright colors make people happy
- **b.** You will be more visible to rescuers
- **c.** Animals are attracted to bright colors
- **d.** Decorating your home always feels nice

77. Straight lines are often found in nature.

- **a.** True
- **b.** False

78. "SOS" stands for:

- **a.** Save Our Souls
- **b.** Save Our Ships
- **c.** Save Our Selves
- **d.** Nothing, it is just the easiest lettering to signal in morse code

79. On a good day, planes can see reflective surfaces from:

- **a.** 20 miles
- **b.** 50 miles
- **c.** 100 miles
- **d.** 300 miles

80. On a map, north is usually oriented:

- **a.** At the bottom
- **b.** On the left
- **c.** On the right
- **d.** At the top

81. A north arrow is usually colored:

- **a.** Blue
- **b.** Red
- **c.** Yellow
- **d.** Green

82. The sun sets in the:

- **a.** North
- **b.** South
- **c.** West
- **d.** East

83. The D in DRSABC of First Aid stands for:

- **a.** Dramatic
- **b.** Danger
- **c.** Dodge
- **d.** Denial

84. Roll a person into the recovery position:

- **a.** If they are tired
- **b.** If they are angry
- **c.** If they are unconscious
- **d.** If they are rude

85. You will need to continue CPR until:

- **a.** The person has started breathing on their own
- **b.** A medical professional has come to take over
- **c.** Your health and safety are compromised
- **d.** Any of the above

86. The best treatment for a serious bleed is:

- **a.** A tourniquet
- **b.** Applying pressure with absorbent material
- **c.** Letting the wound bleed
- **d.** Washing the wound under hot water

87. If a large object is embedded in the wound:

- **a.** Take out the object if the person wants it out
- **b.** Push down hard on the object
- **c.** Leave the object in until you reach medical assistance
- **d.** Wiggle the object a bit to see how badly it's stuck

88. If someone has sprained their ankle, the best treatment is:

- **a.** Rest, ice, compression, elevation
- **b.** Race, ice, compression, elevation
- **c.** Run, exercise, rub, and get on with it
- **d.** Walk it off

89. *Venomous* means:

- **a.** It will make you sick if you eat it
- **b.** It is fast moving
- **c.** If it bites you, then you'll get ill
- **d.** You should never go outdoors

90. The best treatment for a snake bite is:

- **a.** Cut and suck
- **b.** Immobilize the limb and call for help immediately
- **c.** Washing with warm water, as hot as the patient can stand
- **d.** Rub the bite site vigorously

91. The best treatment for a jellyfish sting is:

- **a.** White vinegar and medical assistance
- **b.** Pee on the sting site
- **c.** Wash the tentacles off with water
- **d.** Use your hands to remove the tentacles

92. What is the best thing to treat a burn with?

- **a.** Duck fat
- **b.** Lip balm
- **c.** Olive oil
- **d.** Cold running water

93. You should seek medical help if your burn is larger than:

- **a.** A quarter
- **b.** An inch
- **c.** A palm print
- **d.** A basketball

94. Which of the following is not a symptom of dehydration?

- **a.** Light-colored pee
- **b.** Dry mouth
- **c.** Lack of coordination
- **d.** Dizziness

95. You should do the following as soon as you feel dehydrated:

- **a.** Stop
- **b.** Rest in the shade
- **c.** Hydrate
- **d.** All of the above

96. A cold weather–related condition is:

- **a.** Shingles
- **b.** Hypothermia
- **c.** Hyperthermia
- **d.** Diabetes

97. With a hypothermia patient it is important to:

- **a.** Warm them quickly
- **b.** Give them alcohol
- **c.** Rub them vigorously
- **d.** Warm them slowly and gently

98. When splinting a limb:

- **a.** Put the limb into the position that looks the best
- **b.** Make sure the bandage is tight
- **c.** Support the limb using the position where the patient feels most comfortable
- **d.** Make sure all the joints are at right angles

99. It is important to evacuate a patient yourself, regardless of conditions and injury.

a. True **b.** False

100. The best stretcher is one that is made:

- **a.** Out of branches
- **b.** Out of backpacks
- **c.** Out of whatever is the strongest and lightest material available
- **d.** With colors matching the patient's clothing

QUIZ ANSWERS

1. **The four attitudes of survival are:**

   b. Be positive, be educated, be prepared, be adaptable

2. **Which one of these is something you can change in a survival scenario?**

   b. The fact you're cold

3. **Most people get rescued within:**

   a. One to three days

4. **Part of the fight-or-flight response is:**

   b. A quick burst of adrenaline that allows for extra energy in an emergency situation

5. **Some things to include in your daypack for a day hike would be:**

   d. All of the above

6. **The Rule of 3s is:**

   d. A complex algebra equation

7. **You can last roughly three days without:**

   b. Water

8. **Which of the following is a survival need?**

   a. Fire

9. **Your survival priorities are:**

   b. Shelter, fire, water, food, rescue

10. **Your main survival priority is:**

    c. Dependent on your specific situation

11. **When you first get a knife, it's important that the edge is blunt so you don't cut yourself.**

    b. False

12. **The blood triangle is:**

c. The area you have to be careful to avoid when using a knife

13. **When choosing a knife:**

d. It should fit comfortably in the palm of your hand

14. **If I don't have my knife in its sheath, then I can put it in the ground to protect the blade.**

b. False

15. **It's important to put your knife away if:**

d. All of the above

16. **When passing a knife to another person, make sure:**

d. You hold the knife by the back of the blade and pass it to them handle first

17. **Only a master flintknapper can make a sharp edge out of a rock.**

b. False

18. **If you don't have a blade, you can make a sharp edge out of:**

d. All of the above

19. **How many hours can it take to die in extreme temperatures?**

c. 3

20. **Which one of these is not a way you lose body heat to the environment?**

a. Smoldering

21. **You are safe to camp in a dry creek bed if:**

d. Never

22. **Some things to look out for that'll make shelter-building easier are:**

    d. All of the above

23. **It's better to build a shelter from scratch so that you know it will be a good one:**

    b. False

24. **When building a shelter:**

    c. Take a moment to assess the best shelter so you only need to build it once

25. **What would not be ideal for a shelter?**

    b. Next to running water

26. **The first level of shelter is:**

    b. Your clothing

27. **Which of the following would be the best shelter to build in a cold environment?**

    c. Tepee

28. **You can survive the night in the snow, even if you can't get a fire going.**

    a.True

29. **Roughly how many days can you survive without water?**

    a. 3

30. **Dehydration symptoms can be:**

    d. All of the above

31. **If you want to prevent water loss:**

    c. Stay in the shade

32. **When going into the outdoors, it's always better to carry more water than you think you'll need:**

    a. True

33. **Which one of these is *not* a way to find water in the outdoors?**

c. Walk up a dry creek bed

34. **The best water to drink without treating is:**

a. Rainwater

35. **Most water in the outdoors is safe to drink.**

b. False

36. **The most effective way of making water safe to drink in the outdoors is:**

d. Boiling

37. **Charcoal is good for upset stomachs because:**

b. It absorbs toxins from water

38. **The best combination of materials for a natural water filter are:**

c. Grass, pebbles, sand, charcoal

39. **In a survival scenario, you should always ration your water to a sip.**

b. False

40. **Which of the following animals is known for putting out campfires?**

d. Rhinoceros

41. **Which one of the following isn't a good thing to do when practicing making a fire?**

b. Wait for a windy day

42. **Which one of the following isn't a requirement to make fire?**

a. Marshmallows

43. **Another name for a tinder bundle is:**
    b. Bird's nest

44. **What makes good tinder?**
    d. All of the above

45. **Which one of the following isn't an important part of fire preparation?**
    a. Striking a match

46. **Which type of wood burns slowly and produces good coals?**
    d. Hardwood

47. **Which one of these is not a method of fire making?**
    c. Rhythmic

48. **Which of these methods of making fire is considered a primitive fire making method?**
    b. Friction fire

49. **The percussion method of making fire involves:**
    c. Two things that, when struck together, create a spark

50. **Wood for a friction fire should ideally be:**
    b. Soft, lightweight wood

51. **How many people are the minimum required for the strap drill method of fire making?**
    b. 2

52. **The best material for a fire saw is:**
    c. Bamboo

53. **How long can you last without food?**
    b. 3 weeks

54. **All berries are edible.**

b. False

55. **Some plants to avoid if you can't positively identify them are:**

c. Red plants

56. **Which of the following isn't a step in the Toxin Test?**

a. Cook

57. **If you've become sick from something you have eaten:**

c. Drink a lot of water and try to vomit

58. **Which of these is not a common edible plant?**

d. Oleander

59. **There are poisonous seaweeds.**

b. False

60. **One thing that won't change the way an animal track looks is:**

b. The color of the animal

61. **Droppings are helpful to look at because they can tell you:**

d. All of the above

62. **One thing to think about before hunting an animal is:**

c. Risk versus reward

63. **It's best to avoid eating frogs that are:**

a. Brightly colored

64. **Which of these insects are okay to eat?**

c. Wood grubs

65. **It's okay to eat mollusks if they:**

b. Are attached to rocks when you find them

66. **Which one of these is not an advantage of passive hunting?**

    a. It takes a lot of time

67. **The best trap to set in all survival scenarios is:**

    c. Flexible, depending on your location

68. **Once you're rescued, you should leave your traps and snares set for the next person who comes along:**

    b. False

69. **Which of the following doesn't contribute to a successful deadfall?**

    b. The color of the deadfall

70. **Which of the following is the best trap for birds?**

    b. Arapuca

71. **The best knot for attaching a hook to a line is:**

    b. Fisherman's knot

72. **Primitive hooks can be made out of the following:**

    d. All of the above

73. **When you are active hunting, it is important that you:**

    b. Take note of the wind direction

74. **If you see an animal eating something, then it's okay for you to eat it too.**

    b. False

75. **When you're lost, you have the best chance of being rescued if you:**

    a. Stay where you are

76. **It's important to try to make yourself visible in a survival scenario because:**

    b. You will be more visible to rescuers

77. **Straight lines are often found in nature.**

b. False

78. **"SOS" stands for:**

d. Nothing, it is just the easiest lettering to signal in morse code

79. **On a good day, planes can see reflective surfaces from:**

c. 100 miles

80. **On a map, north is usually oriented:**

d. At the top

81. **A north arrow is usually colored:**

b. Red

82. **The sun sets in the:**

c. West

83. **The D in DRSABC of First Aid stands for:**

b. Danger

84. **Roll a person into the recovery position:**

c. If they are unconscious

85. **You will need to continue CPR until:**

d. Any of the above

86. **The best treatment for a serious bleed is:**

b. Applying pressure with absorbent material

87. **If a large object is embedded in a wound:**

c. Leave the object in until you reach medical assistance

88. **If a person has sprained their ankle, the best treatment is:**

a. Rest, ice, compression, elevation

89. ***Venomous* means:**
 c. If it bites you, then you'll get ill

90. **The best treatment for a snake bite is:**
 b. Immobilize the limb and call for help immediately

91. **The best treatment for a jellyfish sting is:**
 a. White vinegar and medical assistance

92. **What is the best thing to treat a burn with?**
 d. Cold running water

93. **You should seek medical help if your burn is larger than:**
 b. An inch

94. **Which of the following is not a symptom of dehydration?**
 a. Light-colored pee

95. **You should do the following as soon as you feel dehydrated:**
 d. All of the above

96. **A cold weather–related condition is:**
 b. Hypothermia

97. **With a hypothermia patient, it is important to:**
 d. Warm them slowly and gently

98. **When splinting a limb:**
 c. Support the limb using the position where the patient feels most comfortable

99. **It is important to evacuate a patient yourself, regardless of conditions and injury.**
 b. False

100. **The best stretcher is one that is made:**
 c. Out of whatever is the strongest and lightest material available

ABOUT APPLESAUCE PRESS BOOK PUBLISHERS

Applesauce Press creates thoughtfully designed children's books that spark curiosity, creativity, and learning. With a focus on engaging formats and vibrant illustrations, our titles cover a wide range of subjects to educate and delight young readers. As an imprint of HarperCollins Focus, we are dedicated to bringing fresh, beautifully crafted books to families year-round. Learn more at cidermillpress.com.

"Where Good Books Are Ready for Press"
501 Nelson Place
Nashville, Tennessee 37214 USA